Advance Prai.

"Dr. Wilson's book brings hope for teachers by reframing challenges and providing clear, practical tools for developing academic resilience and emotional well-being. This new understanding of the nervous system supports our students and our selves in today's diverse classroom environments. I felt seen and understood as a teacher in a deeply human way."

—**Marie Powder**, elementary school teacher for 27 years

"Until now, understanding Dr. Porges's Polyvagal Theory has been daunting. Debra Em Wilson's interpretation, with analogies such as leaky boats, car alarms, and loaded backpacks, neatly clarifies the seven polyvagal principles. With this book, teachers will be equipped to get in sync with their challenging students and to transform their classrooms into joyful learning centers."

—**Carol Stock Kranowitz**, MA, author of *The Out-of-Sync Child*

"This is the book I've been waiting for! At last, the science and practice of Polyvagal Theory clarified and adapted for the educational setting, which needs it more than ever. This book will be a gift to therapists, educators, and most of all students, for years to come! I look forward to referencing this book again and again."

—**Dr. Christopher Willard**, faculty, Harvard Medical School, author of *Growing Up Mindful*

"During my life in a special education classroom, I remember trying many different interventions to make learning possible for my students. The only times that felt right to me with my students were when we just sat around and I listened to their stories without judgment. I later carried that into my psychotherapy practice with foster and adopted children. The big question was: Why, when we just talk, do things seem to improve? When I heard about Polyvagal Theory and its applications in therapy, I knew without a doubt why listening and keeping someone safe would have such a profound effect on the outcome. Regulation, regulation, regulation became the way out of overwhelm and into a state of underwhelm.

Debra Em Wilson does a wonderful job of bringing the concepts of safety, regulation, and relationship to the forefront for teachers, counselors, and parents. Her book is a must-read for anyone who has children or works with children in any capacity."

—**Stephen J. Terrell**, PsyD, coauthor of *Nurturing Resilience, Helping Clients Move Forward from Developmental Trauma*, developer of Transforming Touch ®, and founder and adoption specialist of Austin Attachment and Counseling Center

"In *The Polyvagal Path to Joyful Learning*, Debra Em Wilson has written a thoughtful, helpful guide to the ways in which we 'think with our bodies.' Teachers, administrators, and parents can all benefit from reading Wilson's informed and insightful book."

—**Annie Murphy Paul**, author of *The Extended Mind*

"This is a truly powerful book. It integrates Polyvagal Theory with educational practice. It is useful not only for educators, but also for others engaged in the learning/transformation journey. What struck me most was that many of our efforts to change organizations stay at the cognitive level. Wilson makes the case that embodied learning needs to occur. Those that are unable to change, to embark on the journey, should not be seen as resisters, but as those who have experienced trauma. The goal is not just to help them find a new story—so they can be active participants in school, in the learning journey—but to embody that story in the nervous system of the person, of the family, and of the broader ecosystem. This is a wonderful book."

—**Professor Sohail Inayatullah**, UNESCO Chair in Futures Studies, Sejahtera Centre for Sustainability and Humanity, Malaysia, and College of Education, Tamkang University, Taipei

THE POLYVAGAL
PATH TO JOYFUL
LEARNING

THE POLYVAGAL PATH TO JOYFUL LEARNING

TRANSFORMING CLASSROOMS ONE NERVOUS SYSTEM AT A TIME

Debra Em Wilson

Foreword by Deb Dana

Norton Professional Books

An Imprint of W. W. Norton & Company
Celebrating a Century of Independent Publishing

This book is intended as a general information resource for teachers and school administrators. It is not a substitute for appropriate training or supervision. Standards of practice and protocol vary in different educational settings and change over time. No technique or recommendation is guaranteed to be effective in all circumstances, and neither the publisher nor the author(s) can guarantee the complete accuracy, efficacy, or appropriateness of any particular recommendation in every respect or in all settings or circumstances.

For information about permission to reproduce selections from this book, write to Permissions, W. W. Norton & Company, Inc., 500 Fifth Avenue, New York, NY 10110

For information about special discounts for bulk purchases, please contact W. W. Norton Special Sales at specialsales@wwnorton.com or 800-233-4830

Manufacturing by Sterling Pierce
Production manager: Gwen Cullen

ISBN: 978-1-324-03052-2

W. W. Norton & Company, Inc., 500 Fifth Avenue, New York, NY 10110
www.wwnorton.com

W. W. Norton & Company Ltd., 15 Carlisle Street, London W1D 3BS

1 2 3 4 5 6 7 8 9 0

To Deb Dana and Leanna Rae for walking the polyvagal path with me and sharing their wisdom, kindness, and lovely ventral energy along the way.

To my family, Robert, Shalea, Daniel, Jessica, and Sarah, for being the sunshine in my universe.

Contents

Acknowledgments   xi
Foreword   xv
Preface   xix

Introduction   3
Chapter 1 **The Friendship That Begins Within**   11
Chapter 2 **The Learning Foundation of Safety and Connection**   27
Chapter 3 **Regulation Through a Polyvagal Lens**   47
Chapter 4 **Resilience, Relationships, and Reality**   61
Chapter 5 **Anchored and Adaptable Learners**   77
Chapter 6 **The Ventral Path to Joyful Learning**   97
Chapter 7 **The Seven Polyvagal Principles for the Classroom**   115

Afterword Coming Full Circle   125
References   129
Index   139

Acknowledgments

When the possibility of writing this book became a reality, Deb Dana and Leanna Rae believed in my voice and encouraged me to begin writing—trusting the words would find their way onto the page.

Thank you to all the early readers who provided feedback on the draft chapter prior to submitting to Norton. Kathy Martens, talented writer and friend, edited the first chapter submission, helping it through the initial steps in the acceptance process.

Most days, I wrote either at the Oro Valley library or found a peaceful spot in a park when the afternoons at the library shifted from its early morning quiet to a bustle of afterschool activity. I'm grateful to Debbie Pederson, my daughter's respite worker, for taking good care of Shalea so I could find my writing groove unencumbered by parental responsibilities.

Developmental editor, Hudson Perigo, brought my vision to life through her expert editing style and love of all things written. When the writing got tough, she clearly outlined the path forward—maintaining her sense of humor all the while!

My engaging weekly meetings with Leanna Rae provided the supportive bridge connecting polyvagal from the mental health field to education. Many of Leanna's insights blossomed within these pages. As every writer knows, there comes a time in the writing process when energy runs low as the finish nears. I'm grateful for Leanna's generous sharing of ventral energy to see me across the finish line.

Monthly meetings with my teacher friend, Marie Powder, provided a valuable teacher's perspective and assurance that I was on a solid path for bringing polyvagal concepts into busy classrooms.

Thank you to the entire Norton team, including Carol C. Collins, Jamie Vincent, Mariah Eppes, Deborah Malmud, Emma Paolini, and the other wonderful individuals who made me feel safe and supported from start to finish. Your professionalism and clear process made writing for Norton a fantastic experience.

A depth of gratitude goes to Dr. Luke van der Laan, Director of the University of Southern Queensland's Professional Studies Doctoral Program, for supervising my dissertation and ensuring the research contributed positively to my consulting work in schools and the field of education. Professor van der Laan helped clarify the format for bringing the layering framework into this project. On our memorable trip to Australia, Luke treated us like family, including hosting a delicious BBQ that my family still talks about to this day!

I appreciate the contribution of Dr. Sohail Inayatullah's CLA framework and am grateful for his support of this project. My son, Daniel, took time out of his busy life to draw the CLA mountain figure and modify as needed to meet the requirements for publication.

To the researchers and authors whose work I've referenced, including Dr. Andrew Martin's Motivation and Engagement Wheel, thank you for advancing the science and returning my email queries.

Thank you to all the incredible administrators, teachers, and support staff that I've worked with throughout the years. Their dedication to the children of the world inspires and humbles me. Mr. Eggers, my high school biology teacher, nurtured my love of science with his endearing teaching style, sense of humor, and cool embroidered lab coat. He's the reason I became a high school biology teacher.

Special thanks to Becky Darst, now retired, for inviting me into her classroom to try out all my new movement routines. I always left her classroom knowing I'd witnessed teaching at its best. I appreciate all the students who have graced my life with their presence. It's an honor to learn right along beside them.

On a personal note, it's our family's and friends' love and support that create the sunshine in our lives. Robert, my life partner, encouraged me to begin this project and provided invaluable insights. Weekends designed to relax and enjoy one another were often spent writing or talking about *the book*. He remained patient, encouraging, and understanding through it all. I'm so fortunate to have him hold my hand and walk beside me—always making sure I feel safe, appreciated, and loved.

Linda Michaels-Spivey, a talented teacher and friend for every season, has seen me through life's ups and downs and ins and outs. Her steadfast support and encouragement with this project kept the writer's block at bay.

John Mollahan, my daughter's cognitive–behavioral therapist, provided monthly check-ins to ensure all was well with the mother–daughter relationship while cheering me on throughout the writing journey.

With regards to the sinking boat story you'll read in the introduction, J.P. and I remain friends after forty-five years. J.P. still loves boats, and cruises the Pacific Northwest waterways from his home port of Whidbey Island, Washington.

I'll be forever grateful to Shalea's healing team of doctors, teachers, therapists, and friends who helped us push beyond perceived limitations, stayed curious, and believed in infinite possibilities.

And finally, to my polyvagal family and Dr. Stephen Porges, developer of the Polyvagal Theory, may this book begin an engaging conversation around the polyvagal campfire.

Foreword

Reading Stephen Porges's *The Polyvagal Theory* was a watershed moment for me. I am a clinician trained in Sensorimotor Psychotherapy, Internal Family Systems, and Tapas Acupressure Technique, with a specialty in working with complex trauma. I love neuroscience and have always brought an understanding of the brain to my clinical work. Learning about Polyvagal Theory helped me look beneath my clients' symptoms to see the science of their suffering, and I became intrigued with bringing this new map of the nervous system into practical application. In the beginning, I experimented with different ways to integrate Polyvagal Theory into my therapy sessions. Clients were willing test pilots and colleagues offered valuable feedback. After much trial and error, I found a way to incorporate polyvagal principles into my sessions and help my clients learn to navigate their lives with a sense of safety.

As I developed a polyvagal approach to clinical work, it became clear that the nervous system was an integral part of the therapy process no matter what modality was being utilized—that in every session, a therapist was engaging with their client's nervous system. In order to introduce a polyvagal perspective, I had to learn to speak the language of the nervous system and create a structure for therapists and clients to engage in nervous system to nervous system communication. Out of necessity, I became a polyvagal translator. My work has now been translated into fourteen languages and I've become known as a primary translator of Polyvagal Theory.

Polyvagal Theory has a universal appeal in that it is not a clinical protocol. It is the science of how we are human, and it can be applied to every aspect of daily living. After years of developing ways to integrate the science of the nervous system into clinical application, I've begun to explore ways to bring Polyvagal Theory to the population I call "curious human beings." Since the nervous system is a common denominator in our human experience, learning how this system works leads to understanding ourselves and others in a new way. When we use the principles of Polyvagal Theory in our daily lives, we can become active operators of our nervous systems, find regulation in everyday moments, and more skillfully meet the larger challenges that are present in our lives.

A polyvagal perspective is now moving beyond the therapy office into medical settings, the business world, leadership programs, mental health organizations, and the academic arena. Debra Em Wilson is one of the pioneers expanding the reach of Polyvagal Theory. In *The Polyvagal Path to Joyful Learning*, she brings her years of experience in the field of education to guide the process of integrating polyvagal principles in a school setting.

I met Debra a number of years ago when she invited me to speak to her S'cool Moves community. From the moment I saw her materials and heard about her journey as an educator and the mother of a child with a constellation of complex challenges, I knew she brought something special to the classroom. Debra has the credentials and the credibility to work with teachers. She knows firsthand what it is like to be in the classroom and the challenges of being a regulated presence for students whose nervous systems are continuously moving in and out of regulation in a search for safety and connection. She understands the essential interconnectedness of regulation and learning.

The seven principles Debra outlines in *The Polyvagal Path to Joyful Learning* take the reader on a journey to understand how to bring Polyvagal Theory into the classroom. Staying true to the polyvagal philosophy that we first have to know our own nervous systems and then can support others in knowing theirs, she expertly presents each principle with activities and reflections for personal awareness, followed by practices to use in the classroom. Debra's dedication to making the school experience safe for every nervous system—adults and children alike—is evident in her writing. Using her wealth of knowledge about schools and students, while honoring the complexities of the teaching environment, Debra Em Wilson has crafted a guide that makes transforming classrooms possible. And true to its title, she makes this a joyful journey. Expertly blending science, stories, and skills, *The Polyvagal Path to Joyful Learning* is an invitation to walk the polyvagal path with Debra as your trusted guide.

Deb Dana
October 2022

Preface

As I facilitated a workshop on the merging of polyvagal science with educational pedagogy, a teacher, arms folded across her chest, interrupted me.

"Who are you and why should we listen to you?"

She had a point. I'd jumped right into unfamiliar material without introducing myself. As a reader of this book, you might well be asking the same question, so let me begin by providing some background.

When Polyvagal Became Personal

"Your daughter is not a typical child. . . . She will never walk, talk, or function in a meaningful way."

This dreaded prognosis, though embedded in a doctor's carefully chosen words of encouragement, sent shock waves through my nervous system. Between the ages of zero and five, my daughter Shalea and I embarked on an epic adventure in search of something that would fix her.

With each new doctor came another demoralizing diagnosis. Living in a rural community, with minimal resources and support for a child with such complex needs as my daughter, I winged it most of the time. I fed Shalea, born without a rooting or sucking reflex, with an eyedropper until I was able to get her reflexes developed. Somehow, I managed to keep her alive each day; but as predicted, she failed to thrive.

By age five, Shalea's list included microcephaly, failure to thrive, cerebral palsy, pervasive developmental delay, cognitive delay (IQ 54), sensory processing disorder, visual processing disorder, growth hormone deficiency, and Russell-Silver syndrome, a rare genetic disorder.

Eventually I managed to assemble a team around her that included a nutritionist, speech and language pathologist, several occupational therapists (each with their own specialty), physical therapist, audiologist, ophthalmologist, behavioral optometrist, listening therapist, and preschool teacher, as well as an array of medical doctors, body workers, and positive friends who propped me up.

It was a time-consuming and exhausting process going from one specialist to another, but the one moment that stands out most for me happened with an occupational therapist after she had taken what felt like forever to observe Shalea. Finally, she turned, squared her gaze at me—as if telling me I needed to paint my kitchen or weed the walkway—and said, "Roll up your sleeves, Mom. You've got work to do."

And work we did. With the insights and therapy protocols from each of her team members, Shalea continued to improve daily. After spending years teetering on the edge of hopelessness, my feet finally felt firmly planted in possibility.

All that hard-won progress had me considering a new wardrobe of superhero capes for Shalea, her healing team, and myself. Then, like Superman exposed to kryptonite, we hit a brick wall.

At age six, during her first visit with a new neurologist, my sense of achievement was quickly deflated like a pricked balloon. The doctor looked at me slack-faced and delivered his bleak prognosis: "All your work is a waste of time. She'll regress to a two-year-old level because her head's too small."

With a deep sigh and no argument, I simply took Shalea's sweet little hand, walked out his office door, and never returned.

Forcing that doctor's hopeless verdict and flat voice out of my head, I moved forward, continuing to celebrate each new accomplishment—including teaching Shalea to read and write.

As Dr. Ransom Stephens shares in his witty neuroscience book, *The Left Brain Speaks, the Right Brain Laughs*:

Before you can innovate, you need to suffer. . . . Every challenge, however trivial or grand, begins with a mix of desire and need— a compulsion to achieve, a problem to solve, and the stress that goes along with the need to solve it ASAP. If the problem doesn't boil up, it will never engage you. (2016, p. 206)

Personal Meets Professional in Unexpected Ways

I began my teaching career cajoling high school biology students into loving science but found myself consistently perplexed at their inability to read and comprehend their textbooks. They were always up for a corny science joke or pun, but doing the deeper work—like reading—not so much. Wanting to get to the core of this, I returned to college to earn a master's degree and become a reading specialist.

By this time, I'd moved on from teaching biology to focus on high school students in an alternative program, many of whom couldn't read past the third grade level. After a five-year run in the program, and eager to intervene earlier in children's lives, I accepted a position as a reading specialist teaching stalled and unresponsive elementary students how to read. As I embarked down this new and hopeful road, diligently applying all the approaches and best practices I'd learned in my studies—I hit another brick wall. I just wasn't seeing the anticipated progress in my students. Why were these children still failing?

Meanwhile, at home, my daughter was showing remarkable improvement. I'd been employing techniques with Shalea that were derived from the fields of occupational therapy, physical therapy, and developmental optometry; and together, we made learning a moving and joyful experience. For instance, she loved bouncing on her mini trampoline while clapping and counting aloud or using her resistance band to stretch out syllables in words while also working on shoulder stability for writing. When Shalea's brain failed to make neural connections, I discovered that enlisting the help of her body through neurodevelopmental movement improved not only her ability to learn, but also her ability to retain what she'd learned.

What if these same protocols could unlock blocked readers in my literacy groups? To test my hunch, I set about finding ways to modify kinesthetic, therapy-based activities and sneak them into reading sessions with my students. As an example, students learned to spell by doing a word tapping activity I created using red and blue tapping sticks to tap out letters with alternating hands—working on spelling, fine-motor skills, visual-motor integration, focus, regulation, and rhythm at the same time. Taking down the wall, brick by brick, my stalled students began making surprising progress, transforming the way I taught and the way my students learned.

Soon, my fellow teachers were stopping me in the hallways and saying, "Whatever you're doing in that room of yours, keep doing it. I'm noticing improved focus, and the lessons I'm teaching are beginning to stick."

Our test scores jumped noticeably by year's end—yes, due in large measure to our great teaching staff and sound literacy practices—but also because neurodevelopmental intervention had created fertile ground in which seeds of learning could sprout. The same activities I'd used with Shalea proved to be the ticket to moving my reading students forward. Who'd have guessed? Per Dr. Stephens's observation, innovation had been born out of an urgent need to solve a problem.

Bringing Neurodevelopmental Interventions to the Classroom

Eventually, maintaining full-time employment and meeting Shalea's constantly changing needs became too difficult. I needed a job with more flexibility to accommodate medical appointments and my expanded role as parent plus medical case worker. And so, with a paltry sum for child support, no retirement account, no paid holidays, no sick days, no perks, no money in the bank, and no common sense, I took the giant leap into the world of self-employment.

For years I traveled around the country, often with my two kids in tow, conducting professional development seminars in large and bustling cities like New York and quaint, small towns like Glendive, Montana. My program, S'cool Moves, has managed to keep French toast on the table and is now heading into 20-plus years of sharing strategies to improve focus, optimize learning, and facilitate collaboration between special and general education programs.

If you toss my personal and professional worlds into a blender and press the max-blend button, that's the perfect metaphor for my life. People often talk about work–life balance. Mine is a blended state, a smoothie of work, parenting, and play. When you parent a child with special needs and you work in education—life is homogenized. No separation.

I'm always reading books and research journals from a variety of fields in hopes of finding nuggets of applicable insights that apply to Shalea's ongoing difficulties as well as the challenges that constantly arise in schools. But I never expected to discover one theory that would bring everything together and blow the top off my metaphorical blender.

Enter Polyvagal Theory

One auspicious day, Leanna Rae, a clinical social worker from Ft. Worth, Texas, contacted me shortly after attending one of my training courses. During our online meeting, using her best social worker skills, she made me feel safe, encouraged, and supported with benevolent energy. She told me how much she'd enjoyed the course and that the information complemented her work with parents and children struggling in the school system. Then, the opening she'd waited for appeared, and she gracefully sauntered in.

"I think there's more you need to understand about the nervous system. The model you use in your course is an outdated one."

"That's interesting," I said. "Tell me more."

"Have you heard of Polyvagal Theory?"

"Doesn't sound familiar."

Leanna went on to tell me about Dr. Stephen Porges, the scientist who developed Polyvagal Theory, and about Deb Dana, a social worker whose books focus on the practical application of Porges's work. She even offered to connect me with Deb Dana and suggested she'd be a great person for me to interview on my monthly podcast.

"Sounds great," I said, with no idea that my life-smoothie was about to get a blast of superpowered, cell-nourishing, brain-enhancing nutrients.

After the meeting I immediately began researching everything we'd talked about. I ordered Deb Dana's book, *The Polyvagal Theory in Therapy: Engaging the Rhythm of Regulation*. I devoured it, sticking flags on just about every other page to note key concepts.

The Interview and the Fork in the Road

Deb Dana graciously agreed to be interviewed on my show. At the time, I had no idea of her rock star status as a prolific author, clinician, and consultant in the field of social work. I just knew that I loved her book and marveled at how she'd managed to explain, simplify, and personalize complex neuroscience focusing on the autonomic nervous system.

During our interview, as I asked questions from a teacher's perspective, a whole new world unfolded with each of her calm, thoughtful responses. Through a polyvagal lens, all the wins and losses with both Shalea and my students started to make so much more sense. My understanding began to deepen as to why certain strategies worked and others didn't—why I was more successful with some students and not as much with others.

At one point, the interview turned personal, and I briefly shared my childhood story of life-threatening domestic violence and witnessing a mother too clinically depressed to leave. Deb radiates warmth and kindness that makes you feel like it's just the two of you in the room and safe to share, even if you have a hundred listeners on the line. She compassionately reframed my experiences within the context of Polyvagal Theory, and in doing so helped me realize that we take our nervous systems (and all the experiences that have shaped them) with us wherever we go—including into our classrooms. With this one interview, a fork in the road appeared, and I took the path that has made all the difference in how I parent and how I teach. Inspired, I wanted to share what I'd learned with my colleagues.

Polly Who?

During an online training session with a leadership team from a school in Northern California, a teacher stopped me during my compressed introduction to Polyvagal Theory and asked, "Now how do you spell her name? I got Polly, but how do you spell her last name?"

That's when I knew that a brief, 20-minute scratch-the-surface explanation of Dr. Porges's theory wasn't the best way to go. My already jam-packed six-hour course focusing on teacher and support staff collaboration didn't allow more time. But I also knew that the role the nervous system plays in teaching and learning warranted greater attention and had the power to transform classrooms. In a classroom of diverse students, the common denominator is that everyone is affected by the state of their nervous systems. And it's in understanding this marvelous system that we can change classrooms (and the world) one nervous system at a time (Dana, 2018).

With encouragement from my colleagues in the field of social work, I wanted to bring Polyvagal Theory—already prominent in the clinical disciplines of psychology, counseling, and social work—into today's complex and often challenging teaching environments. Hence this book.

By the way, in case you're wondering, the word *polyvagal* comes from the Greek prefix *poly*, meaning more than one, and the vagus nerve, which comes from the Latin word for *wandering*. You'll read all about the wandering nerve in Chapter 1.

THE POLYVAGAL
PATH TO JOYFUL
LEARNING

Introduction

You do a lot of good things for students in your classroom. You attend professional development, create professional learning communities, stay abreast of advances in your subject area, and read the continuing scroll of information online as your administration adopts one curriculum after another in a never-ending quest to find solutions to ever-increasing challenges. You can feel swamped. And to keep your "teaching boat" afloat, you attempt to plug holes with whatever's within arm's reach.

It's like the sunbaked, dilapidated 1958 Islander, a 24-foot wooden sailboat my college boyfriend purchased with dreams of restoring. Perched on dry dock stands, she longingly awaited her return home to the sea after years of neglect. We camped underneath the Islander and worked together sanding and repairing as time allowed between classes and work schedules.

Finally, caulking between her diagonal wood planking and plugging holes, we were confident she'd float. We hired a boat-moving service to take her to the closest place for launching, a harbor where mostly upscale and elite yachts spent their days. Held aloft by a boat-lift sling and being slowly lowered into the water, our modest sailboat garnered curiosity from the yacht crowd, and an audience began to form, martinis in hand.

At last, she reached the water. While our pride swelled, the boat's planks unfortunately did not. Port to starboard, water came flooding in from every nook and cranny.

There's an old expression in the nautical world that the best bilge pump is a scared man and a bucket. We jumped onto the boat, grabbed our buckets, and frantically began tossing water overboard. The crowd looked on, some laughing and others showing a bit more compassion for our situation, but not sure how to help. At the same time, it started to rain.

Do you find some days are like that at school? You grab your bucket and try to keep your little boat afloat while water rushes in. After reading this book, you might find that Polyvagal Theory is the caulking that fills the cracks in your planking so you can do less bailing and more sailing.

While conducting research for this book, I read many densely packed tomes full of impressive terms from experts specializing in a variety of education and education-related topics such as trauma, social–emotional learning, behavior, social sciences, and neuroscience. Current neuroscience research is finding that the brain has limits (Paul, 2021), and I'd reached my capacity.

Gary Keller, author of the *Wall Street Journal* best-selling book, *The One Thing*, poses the question, "What is the one thing I can do such that by doing it everything else will be easier or unnecessary?" (2012, p. 8).

If I were asked what my one thing is, undoubtably it would be the application of Polyvagal Theory in our classrooms and our lives. It's the one thing that can make everything else you do easier and lighten your cognitive load.

What Exactly Is Polyvagal Theory?

Dr. Stephen Porges is a professor of psychiatry at the University of North Carolina and a distinguished university scientist at Indiana University, including his role as director of the Traumatic Stress Research Consortium. He first introduced Polyvagal Theory to the Society for Psychophysiological Research in 1995 (Porges, 2017) and has since published in a variety of scientific journals and authored several books on the topic.

Polyvagal Theory focuses on the functions of the body's autonomic nervous system (ANS) and posits that:

- There is a bidirectional link between the brain and body—thoughts change physiology, and physiology changes thoughts.

- Connecting and regulating with other humans are biological imperatives, essential for survival.
- Feeling safe is the most important variable in the successful treatment of mental health issues, behavior challenges, and trauma. (Porges, 2021)

The theory found traction when practitioners translated the scientific explanations into applicable frameworks, techniques, and exercises that deepened current therapeutic interventions (Badenoch, 2018; Dana, 2018; Kain & Terrell, 2018; Tronick & Gold, 2020). It continues to grow in popularity within the fields of social work, mental health, and counseling due to its successful contributions to understanding the nervous system's role in regulation and well-being.

You probably know that the ANS takes care of many physiological functions you don't have to think about, including heartbeat, body temperature, and digestion. In addition, it's also your built-in bodyguard, on alert for signals of safety and danger (what Deb Dana calls "cues") from people and the environment. Your ANS responds in three distinct ways:

1. It allows you to feel safe enough to engage in the daily trials, tribulations, and celebrations of life while staying connected to yourself and others.
2. It mobilizes you into action so that you can fight or run from the threat of danger.
3. It immobilizes you when the threat of danger is too great, and shutdown is deemed the best course for survival.

If you're under constant stress or have experienced emotional trauma, this system may become overresponsive when danger is perceived. Often the threat is based more on past experiences than on the current situation, which might be quite safe. It's like a car alarm that goes off every time someone walks by. Finding regulation is difficult when the ANS constantly feels threatened.

This has profound implications in the classroom, where you may have students whose nervous systems are like that car alarm, constantly poised to send signals of danger. These signals come from inside themselves, outside in the environment, or in relationships with others (Dana, 2018). Through the application of Polyvagal Theory, students learn how to understand their nervous systems, bringing more predictability and choices when responding to challenges and, in doing so, becoming more flexible and elastic—ultimately, more resilient and adaptable. The focus isn't on healing trauma but rather about offering opportunities for the nervous system to learn how to engage, disengage, and reengage (Dana, 2018). This is done through neural exercises (activities that help us become active operators of our nervous systems) designed to increase nervous system flexibility by offering cues of safety and connection (Dana, 2018; Porges, 2017).

When you understand Polyvagal Theory and the role of the nervous system in learning, your classrooms can become environments that increase staff and student well-being by developing skills leading to increased resilience, adaptability, and flexibility—essential qualities for social, emotional, and academic success.

Is Polyvagal Theory Evidence Based?

Absolutely. Like everything scientific, what we know changes over time. This is the case for Polyvagal Theory as well. A theory is merely an idea expanded through facts, principles, and scientific explanation. As I type these words and by the time this book is published, some of the information may have already changed due to advances in science. I can only write what is known now based on the evidence presented in support of Porges's Polyvagal Theory.

As the theory grows in popularity, there are some detractors, but Dr. Porges diligently responds to criticisms and misunderstandings of his theory as they crop up. Most criticisms are based in the details of physiology—the common person on the street wouldn't have any idea what the discussions are all about. What is presented in this book are concepts that are widely published in peer-reviewed journals; accepted in the mental health, social work, and medical fields; and emerging in the field of education.

Polyvagal Theory has its own unique language, created by Dr. Stephen Porges and Deb Dana—and it originates from the biological sciences. By book's end, you'll be speaking polyvagal for the classroom like a native. And while we will be discussing the theory's basic terms, those wanting to learn expansive polyvagal terminology and accompanying scientific definitions should refer to *The Pocket Guide to the Polyvagal Theory* (Porges, 2017).

In the upcoming chapters, you'll learn how the different states of your students' nervous systems, collectively as a group and individually, inform interventions and impact outcomes in your classroom.

Programs Come and Go, But Your Nervous System Is Here to Stay

Polyvagal Theory isn't a fad or a program, but rather a framework to understand and optimize the learning experience. Every student we work with and every child we parent is different, but there's one thing they all have in common—a responsive nervous system ready for action. This is something upon which we can all agree. Understanding and applying Polyvagal Theory is the perfect starting point, as it underpins many of the programs we currently use in classrooms.

Deb Dana writes, "My personal experience, and my experience teaching Polyvagal Theory to therapists and clients is that there is a before-and-after quality to learning this theory. Once you understand the role of the autonomic nervous system in shaping our lives, you can never again not see the world through that lens" (2018, p. xix).

By understanding how the ANS responds throughout the day, you can create transformative learning environments where children and the adults who mentor them work together and optimize the synergistic relationship between the mind, body, and environment.

A No-Stress Approach to Learning Polyvagal Theory

Knowing the reality of teaching and parenting in today's busy times, I've organized this book into seven chapters. Each chapter focuses on an overarching polyvagal principle so you can proceed at your own pace, taking it one chapter at a time.

The objective of Chapter 1 is to help you observe and develop an intimate friendship with your own nervous system. Befriending your nervous system requires an understanding of the concept of *hierarchy*—a predictable way your nervous system responds to perceived safety or threat. This understanding begins your polyvagal journey and is the important first step to applying Polyvagal Theory in your classroom.

Chapter 2 defines and illustrates the concept of *neuroception*—the way your nervous system, without your conscious awareness, evaluates risk by assessing signals of safety and danger that come from inside your body, the outside environment, and relationships with others (Porges, 2017). We explore the importance of safety and connection—concepts often overlooked in the immediacy of finding solutions to behavior challenges and learning issues.

We'll investigate the relationship between nervous system states and the cognitive stories our minds create to make sense of those states (often called personal narratives) as they form a bidirectional loop, with one affecting the other. You'll discover the deeper layers that underpin personal narratives, as well as what Deb Dana calls the Three Cs of Safety, which are at the center of the state and story relationship.

In Chapter 3, we discover why *co-regulation* is a biological imperative beginning with the mother–infant relationship, and essential before children can self-regulate. Regulation is viewed through a polyvagal lens and expanded to include the concept of *interactive regulation*. We will enhance our understanding of the essential need for co-regulation as well as self-regulation by weaving important polyvagal concepts into the research focusing on self-regulated, co-regulated, and shared regulated learning.

Chapter 4 focuses on the important topic of resilience and its role in student achievement. Polyvagal Theory is integrated into research highlighting the internal and external protective factors leading to *academic resilience*. The reparative continuum is an important polyvagal concept that goes hand-in-hand with creating positive relationships, optimizing learning, and developing resilience. You'll learn about triggers and glimmers within the context of micromoments—those tiny units of time when the magic really happens.

Chapter 5 deepens your understanding of the three nervous system states (ventral vagal, sympathetic, and dorsal vagal) and what happens when states become blended. You'll discover your default state and explore ways to help yourself stay or get back to a place where you are able to remain sure-footed during challenging situations in life and in the classroom.

Chapter 6 synthesizes everything learned in the previous chapters and highlights polyvagal-guided strategies to ensure that students are ready to learn (and remember) all that good stuff we teach.

The concepts of Polyvagal Theory are integrated into the mindset paradigm and academic learning theories. Three forms of cognition are introduced and woven into polyvagal concepts including *embodied cognition* (inside the body), *situated cognition* (optimizing the environment), and *distributed cognition* (working collaboratively with others).

By Chapter 7, you'll be on the path to joyful learning and speaking polyvagal like a native. A review of the seven principles along with suggestions for bringing the principles alive will move you forward on your polyvagal journey.

. . .

The experiences that have shaped your nervous system influence how you respond to events and challenges at home, and at school. Though you often think of your work and home lives as being separate, the reality is that you bring your nervous system (complete with all the history and over-stuffed satchels from your past) to work with you every day. Befriending your nervous system and helping students befriend theirs is where your polyvagal adventure begins. Let's take a collective deep breath, find some quiet time to spend with each other, and connect through these pages—writer and reader on a journey of discovery together.

CHAPTER 1

The Friendship That Begins Within

After a long night caring for my two children (both of whom had miserable colds), I arrived at school bright and early to fulfill my morning-duty obligations. Out in the freezing cold, snowflakes gathered in my hair. As the morning bell rang and freed me from my Arctic tarmac misery, I trudged into my classroom exhausted from no sleep and in a foul mood.

When my students came charging through the door, the ranting began: "I've told you not to run in the hallways. You know what you need to do when you come through this door. Inside *my* classroom you behave . . . " and on and on it went. I continued to find fault with everything the students did or didn't do.

Finally, not being able to take any more of my nonsense, a sweet student voice from the back of the room said, "Ms. Wilson, I think you're having a bad day. You need to do your calming routine. It'll help!"

The Promise of Polyvagal Theory

At some time or another, you've been in one of *those* moods. We are, after all, humans in the classroom first and students, teachers, and support staff second. It's when these feelings persist and we can't find a way back to a place of equanimity that we hit the tipping point and join the ranks of other professionals heading out the education door. Dr. Patricia Jennings (2021) explains her observations this way:

> For the past twenty years, I have been carefully following the teacher burnout crisis and watching as each year the attrition rate increases. We have now reached a cross-roads; the exodus of teachers from the profession is real and growing, and the problem is threatening to unravel our education systems across the country and around the world. (p. 1)

A colleague once told me that burnout represents not using your resources wisely, and that a more accurate term for how she felt was not *burned out*, but rather *disillusioned*. One of the promising ways to renew hope and ward off teacher exodus is by understanding the role the nervous system plays in determining how you feel about your work and personal life. With understanding comes a deeper appreciation of how your nervous system responds when you're feeling overwhelmed, and self-care falls low on the priority list. When you're in a place of fight, flight, or despair, there are fewer options, fewer solutions, fewer "aha" insights, fewer moments of seeing what's working and what may be possible. On my no-good-very-cranky-day, I was seeing more obstacles than options. It was a wise student who reminded me of the value of taking a few moments to regulate, care for myself, and move through feeling tired and disillusioned.

In education (and most helping professions) there's a tendency to regard nourishing oneself as something there's just not enough time to do. I once overheard a teacher say, "If I hear my principal use the words self-care, building relationships, compassion, or resiliency one more time. . . . " It's easy to become cynical when such vague concepts are tossed around as if educators have a bucket full of leftover hours to burn on what might be perceived as best suited for the counseling room. Piled on top of all you're already doing, living up to these expectations can seem an impossible task.

Yet focusing on yourself and specifically your nervous system is the way forward. So let's jump right in with the first of the seven principles designed to positively impact your life inside and outside the classroom.

PRINCIPLE ONE: Befriend your nervous system.

"Befriend your nervous system" is an expression coined by Deb Dana—a kind and gentle way to increase awareness of this system within you that is constantly monitoring the environment for signs of safety and danger. Who you are in the world is largely determined by how your autonomic nervous system (ANS) is interpreting what you feel inside, what is going on outside in your environment, and what's happening between yourself and others. Moment by moment there is a physiological bidirectional dance going on between your mind and body, your body and mind.

To understand and apply Polyvagal Theory in your classroom, it's important for you to first befriend your own nervous system. This journey isn't a top-down, cognitive experience—it's an inside-out exploration. There's a sense of urgency in education and a need for quick fixes in the classroom, but befriending is a process that takes time. Resist the urge to move on to the other chapters before completing the activities in this one, as they are the underpinnings of everything yet to come.

Shelley Taylor, a UCLA psychologist, uses the phrase "tend and befriend" to explain that our nervous system has developed not only survival responses but also a strong, consistent need to nurture and care for others (Paul, 2021). If not kept in check, nurturing others comes at the expense of caring for ourselves. By befriending your nervous system, you are more able to practice self-care, maintain energy for work, and nurture positive friendships—all fuel for keeping the spark lit that initially brought you into the teaching profession in the first place.

Lydia Denworth (2020), a science journalist and the author of the book *Friendship*, describes friendship as a matter of life and death, carried with us from generation to generation in our DNA. We're wired for social bonding. Friendship is not a choice or a luxury; it's an absolute essential for happiness and thriving.

The same imperative for friendship can be applied to the idea of befriending your nervous system. According to Denworth, "[the term] *friend* carries emotional weight, signifying something about the quality and character of a relationship that is based on history and the content of repeated interactions" (2020, p. 140). Similarly, it's your history and repeated interactions in your environment (including relationships) that have shaped your nervous system. Through the befriending process, you can become intimately acquainted with your own nervous system and cultivate a lasting friendship that stands the test of time. A quick science lesson is in order, so warm up a cup of coffee as we begin the introduction.

A Quick-Start Introduction to Your Nervous System

Every hour, every minute, every second, your nervous system is at work helping you negotiate each day as healthy and unscathed as possible. To illustrate, if you did indeed get yourself a cup of coffee in preparation for this discussion, and the cup overheated in the microwave—your nervous system sent a signal from receptors in your skin to your brain that your cup was too hot. Your nervous system then sent you another, more urgent message, saying, "Too hot! Drop the cup!" You quickly put the cup on the counter, let out a yelp, and realized your fingers were a bit burned. You turned on the faucet and ran your hand under cold water while thinking you really need to invest in some insulated cups.

Though the term *nervous system* is often thought of as singular, several systems in your body worked together in response to the hot coffee cup—informing you of potential danger and keeping you as safe as possible. Let's examine this amazing tangle of sophisticated circuitry (Figure 1.1).

The nervous system consists of:

1. the central nervous system, which includes your brain and spinal cord, and
2. the peripheral nervous system, which resides primarily outside the central nervous system.

The peripheral nervous system consists of the *sensory and motor divisions*. In the case of the hot coffee cup, the sensory division of the PNS sent information to the brain that the cup was hot. The brain then relayed a message to the motor division to release the cup quickly to avoid getting burned.

The motor division divides further into the *somatic nervous system* and the ANS. The somatic nervous system is responsible for voluntary control

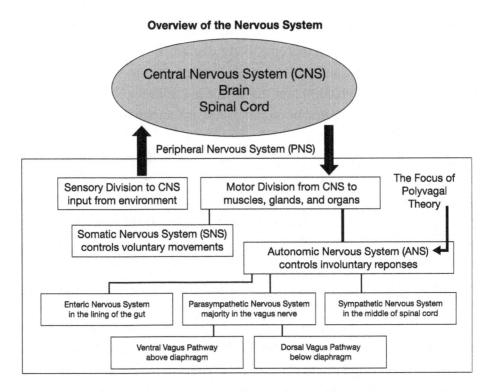

Overview of the Nervous System

FIGURE 1.1   OVERVIEW OF THE NERVOUS SYSTEM

of your body by way of your skeletal muscles. Voluntarily turning on the water when your hand felt burned is an example of the somatic nervous system in action. You consciously initiated the movement.

The ANS is the focus of Polyvagal Theory and consists of three subsystems: *enteric, sympathetic*, and *parasympathetic nervous systems*. These three systems work harmoniously together to aid in breathing, heart rate, digestion, and other unconscious functions.

In the case of the hot coffee cup, the ANS was working in the background to detect the level of threat and respond to the degree of perceived danger. When the ANS detects a threat of some kind, it shifts from a steady state into activation. Since you weren't in grave danger, the ANS kept a low profile and didn't engage in any life-saving measures.

Now to the All-Important Vagus Nerve

Rather than being a single nerve, the *vagus* is a bundle of nerve fibers communicating bidirectionally between the body and the brain. If you're up on your Latin (and who isn't?), you'll recognize that *vagus* roughly translates as *wandering*, which perfectly describes the vagus nerve as it wanders throughout the body—from the brain stem to the colon. While the sympathetic nervous system resides in the middle of the spinal cord, most of the parasympathetic nervous system accompanies the vagus nerve as it traverses its merry way.

Of remarkable note is that 80% of vagus nerve fibers are sensory and relay messages to the brain, while only 20% of vagus nerve fibers are motor, sending action information from the brain to the body (Dana, 2018; Porges, 2017). This means the vagus nerve, with its unique ratio of sensory to motor nerve fibers, is primarily wired to receive sensory information related to your well-being.

The vagus nerve has two response pathways: the *ventral vagus* and the *dorsal vagus* pathways. These pathways are the largest component of the body's parasympathetic system. The ventral and dorsal vagal fibers exit the brain stem together but end up in different locations in the body—with the ventral vagal fibers claiming territory above the diaphragm and the dorsal vagal fibers below the diaphragm. The ventral vagal fibers are designed for faster nerve conduction and the dorsal vagal fibers for slower transmission speed. We'll discuss the significance of this a bit later.

Updating the Old Model of the ANS

Armed with this knowledge, you've reached your polyvagal destination—a new interpretation of how the ANS responds to stimuli. Now the exciting polyvagal journey really begins!

The common but outdated model of the sympathetic and parasympathetic nervous systems is an either/or response to stimuli, focusing on the concept of paired antagonism. This model, which was taught for centuries, represents a black-and-white duality of two opposing responses:

1. sympathetic (mobilization through the commonly known as *fight-or-flight response*), or
2. parasympathetic (immobilization through *rest and digest*).

Polyvagal Theory posits that when a life-threatening situation is detected, the parasympathetic nervous system (via the vagus nerve's dorsal vagus pathway) may also initiate a third response, causing you to shut down.

One of the important contributions of the newer ANS model to clinical therapy is that it offers a way to explain reactions to extreme trauma through understanding the role of the dorsal vagus pathway and its response to life-threatening situations.

Before Polyvagal Theory, there was no way of telling the story of the body shutting down, nor of understanding the nervous system's response to truly life-threatening situations, no way to understand why sometimes we can't run or fight back. We do more than freeze in the moment. We are immobilized and shutdown. And we may suffer long-term, intrinsic consequences of those responses.

With the discovery of the division within the parasympathetic nervous system, there is now a biological explanation for why we become immobilized—even when over time our conscious selves believe that we should've stood up to the threat and fought back harder. We should've run faster or tried harder to avoid the danger. Biologically, in response to truly life-threatening situations, the involuntary dorsal vagus response can shut the body down for protection and in service of survival. This response isn't recognized in the former model of the ANS.

There are three overarching concepts of Polyvagal Theory: hierarchy, neuroception, and co-regulation (Dana, 2018). In this chapter, we'll focus on hierarchy and cover the other two concepts in upcoming chapters. The world is an unpredictable and sometimes unsafe place—you can't control all the events that come at you each day. Yet you can take some control of your ANS by understanding and thus predicting how it will operate. It's in the concept of hierarchy that we find predictability and begin taking an active role in the operation of our nervous system.

Hierarchy and the Autonomic Ladder

The term *hierarchy* is used to describe the orderly response pattern from the newest to oldest evolutionary pathways (Porges, 2017). As you recall, there are three ANS pathways: ventral vagus, sympathetic, and dorsal vagus. The ventral vagus pathway is the newest pathway to have evolved. The sympathetic pathway evolved before that. The dorsal vagus pathway

FIGURE 1.2   THE AUTONOMIC LADDER (Adapted from THE POLYVAGAL THEORY IN THERAPY: ENGAGING THE RHYTHM OF REGULATION by Deb Dana. Copyright © 2018 by Deb Dana. Used by permission of W. W. Norton & Company, Inc.)

is the oldest evolutionary pathway. Deb Dana's ladder metaphor can depict the hierarchy of the ANS in responding from the newer pathways to the oldest (Figure 1.2).

The ANS responses are referred to as *states*. At the top of the ladder, you're in a *ventral vagal state*. In the middle of the ladder, you're in a *sympathetic state*. The bottom rung of the ladder is called a *dorsal vagal state*. Individual response times of nerve fibers also play a role in hierarchy. The faster ventral vagus and sympathetic nerve fibers are the first and second responders, respectively. The dorsal vagus nerve fibers are the slowest to respond, which is the reason why the dorsal vagal is at the bottom of the ladder, the last response in the hierarchy. Let's bring this information to life through a polyvagal story that demonstrates how the states-of-response hierarchy works. Finally, something in life that's predictable!

The Ventral Vagal State

Imagine a blissful picnic beside a meandering pastoral stream. You're surrounded by a rainbow of wildflowers under a cooling green canopy of fresh spring leaves. You're relaxed and enjoying the sights and sounds of nature while reading the current best-seller, *An Educator's Guide to Infinite Time and Wisdom.* You are at the top of the ladder in the ventral vagal state. Suddenly, out of a grove of trees lumbers a large, foraging black bear.

If by some miracle you recall that, unlike other species, black bears rarely attack people—you will stay in a ventral vagal state. You tell yourself that you're likely quite safe. The bear sniffs a bit, decides you're uninteresting, and rambles on. Slightly annoyed but relatively unfazed, you remain calm and go back to reading and enjoying your day.

The Sympathetic State

Your nervous system may have other ideas about this bear situation. It's decided that the threat of danger is too great, and that you need to act now! Your sympathetic response is activated, and you're moving out of a ventral vagal state and poised for any contingency (moving down the ladder). Your sympathetic nervous system responds to the danger in one of two ways: fight or flight. If it's flight—you toss your book aside and run like the dickens to get away. If it's fight—you stand up to the bear by making yourself appear really big and banging on some pots, if you just happen to have some lying around. If this doesn't work, the flight response comes back online, encouraging your feet to put some serious distance between you and *Ursus americanus.*

After the threat has passed and you're on the way back to a ventral vagal state (heading back up the ladder), your heart rate eventually returns to normal, and the sympathetic activation system calms. Now you're thinking clearly and can decide what to do next (back to the top of the ladder): leave your lunch for the bear to enjoy, pack up your picnic basket and call it a day, or stay and enjoy the sunset. After all, what are the odds of seeing two bears in one day?

The Dorsal Vagal State

What happens when your nervous system perceives the situation as life threatening, and the alarm bells ring inside you? Your sympathetic nervous system tries to engage, but it's overridden by your parasympathetic dorsal response because the threat is perceived as too great and too dangerous (bottom rungs of the ladder). You try to move, but you can't. You've moved into dorsal vagal shutdown. Unable to fight or flee, you curl up into a ball and become very quiet—and still hoping that the bear partakes of your sandwich and not you, then takes his satiated self back to the trees from whence he came.

In dorsal vagal shutdown, your nervous system must find a way to mobilize you toward the sympathetic state before you can find your way back to the ventral vagal state of safety. Fortunately, you hear the footsteps of a friendly park ranger who witnessed the tail end of the ruckus and has come to see if you're okay. Feeling safe enough to come out of the dorsal vagal state and connect with another human, you slowly move, accept a helping hand from the ranger, stand up, and begin to find your way back to the ventral vagal state (moving through the center rungs of the ladder). You've engaged with nature enough for one day, pack up your picnic, and head to the nearest café, where you think to yourself, "Picnics in nature are highly overrated!"

The Autonomic Ladder in the Classroom

While the bear story takes place outside the classroom, your nervous system's hierarchy of responses to situations inside your classroom is similar. You move up and down your Autonomic Ladder throughout the day, whether you're dealing with a student's behavior issue, a fight breaking out on the playground, or an impromptu fire drill—your nervous system analyzes the degree of threat and responds accordingly.

The more you understand and befriend your nervous system, the better you'll be able to handle daily challenges in your classroom without being exhausted by day's end. Based on your nervous system states, the world can be a safe, supportive place or dangerous and unsupportive. Let's explore how the world looks from different states of the nervous system.

The View From the Ventral Vagal State

A visual mnemonic to help you remember the ventral state is a heart with a vent that represents all the good stuff you let in and give out when you are in a good relationship with yourself, the environment, others, nature, and spirit (whatever that might personally mean for you). This is often referred to as *ventral energy*. When you bring ventral energy to all the associated experiences that being in a classroom offers, the feeling is one of abundance rather than scarcity. You're able to discover additional untapped resources inside yourself, in your environment, and in your students.

In the ventral vagal state, you feel safe to engage with others and handle the inherent ups and downs that are part of living in this world. The feelings associated with the ventral vagal state include but are not limited to safety, relaxation, passion, curiosity, connection, regulation, and a sense that while things may not be perfect, they're okay. And that's enough to keep you on your ventral path.

In the ventral vagal state, the world is a supportive and welcoming place. You feel grounded, safe enough to connect with others, inspired to learn new things, able to see obstacles clearly, express compassion, and handle the little and not so little challenges that arise.

In the classroom, the ventral vagal state is the optimal state for learning. It's one of safety, connection, and infinite possibilities.

The View From the Sympathetic State

To remember the sympathetic state, visualize a runner and a fighter while embracing the irony that the word itself is the opposite of how you feel. Sympathetic resources like compassion, understanding, and empathy aren't available to you when you're in a sympathetic state. In the language of Polyvagal Theory (which, remember, comes from the biological sciences), you can't be sympathetic in a sympathetic state!

Life looks very different from the sympathetic vantage point. In the sympathetic state, the world is threatening, and you don't put much faith in your fellow humans. People are more often foe than friend. Experiences are perceived as risky and unpredictable. You are mobilized for a fight-or-flight response. This mobilization may be organized to get you out of the perceived danger, or it may be disorganized—you know you need to get out of the situation but you're not sure where the exit is located.

In the sympathetic state, you're flooded with mobilizing energy, unable to see people as benevolent beings, and unable to care about others (unsympathetic!). You are dysregulated. In this state the world is dangerous, unpredictable, and threatening. You may feel anxious, overwhelmed, untrusting, or irrationally afraid.

Students in sympathetic states are mobilized for action, but the mobilization is coming from a place of disorganization—fight or flight. It's difficult to focus when in a sympathetic state. These students mobilize from a place of fear and exhibit survival energy, poised for pushing back, challenging, or escaping whatever you've planned for the day.

The View From the Dorsal Vagal State

To help you remember the responses common to a dorsal vagal state, visualize a door closing out the world. From the dorsal vagal vantage point, you experience life-threatening cues of danger and lack energy to move forward. You want to disconnect from the world or even disappear completely. The feelings associated with the dorsal vagal state include collapse, loneliness, numbness, dissociation, hopelessness, fogginess, or feeling untethered.

In the dorsal vagal state, the world is a lonely place, unsafe and unsupportive. You may feel despair, disconnection from others, or may want to become invisible or not be in the world at all. Noticing these states in yourself and your students is the first step in applying Polyvagal Theory.

Students in a dorsal vagal state may be collapsed in their seats with poor posture, checked-out, sleepy, or stuck in a why-bother pattern and unable to learn. These students tend to be overlooked in classrooms because they aren't loud and noticeable. These are the quietly failing students, discussed at length in Chapter 5.

You may use a favorite discipline, regulation, or social–emotional learning program to support students in any response state; however, understanding the hierarchy of these responses can make the programs you already use that much more powerful. Applying Polyvagal Theory doesn't replace your tried-and-true programs, but rather enhances them.

And the more you understand your nervous system, the better you'll be able to understand your students and choose the most appropriate methods of support.

Being Patient With the Befriending Process

It's easy to judge, get frustrated, and expect more than your nervous system is ready to give. Remember, befriending means observing with curiosity rather than judgment. You navigate your life based on prior experiences or the response patterns that align with familiarity. Through befriending your nervous system, you'll be better able to manage all the challenges that life throws at you each day.

Mother Teresa compassionately stated, "We can do no great things, only small things with great love." We make change by doing little things over and over. Great things are done by a series of small things brought together in a moment. It's in the micromoments that the shift begins to happen. Be kind to your nervous system; reach inside with compassion and make incremental changes. Do so with great love for yourself.

Self-care and self-kindness don't need to be expensive massages or weekend getaways at a healing retreat. There are many small but powerful ways to bring self-care into your school day. For example:

- Wear your favorite warm and comfy sweater.
- Hang a nature poster for when you need a moment of beauty.
- Bring in a live plant that you and your students can nurture.
- Play a fun song and move with your students.
- Turn a worksheet into an art project.
- Reach out to a colleague for a few minutes after school—just to share and connect.
- Help your students find bright spots in the day and allow time to express them.

Only when you show yourself the same kindness you show your friends are you able to bring your regulated nervous system to work, be present with your students, and find solutions to challenging situations that confront you between the wee hours of the morn until tucking yourself into bed at night. "Being kind to yourself is one of the greatest kindnesses," says the mole in the beautiful *New York Times* best-seller, *The Boy, the Mole, the Fox, and the Horse* (Mackesy, 2019).

You move in and out of your nervous system states several times throughout the day. The objective is not to be in a ventral vagal state every moment, but to observe when you're wandering off your ventral path and keep ventral in view.

Though not always easy, befriending your nervous system is an essential process for bringing a regulated nervous system to work. Your students look to you for guidance on how to be their best selves. They're watching, learning, and imitating. "You are the social leader of the classroom, and your students will follow your lead when it comes to relating to other students in the classroom" (Jennings, 2019b, p. 55). One of the best ways to lead is by befriending your nervous system and being a regulated adult in the classroom.

Take the befriending process with you into Chapter 2, where you're introduced to an effective framework for understanding how your mind creates the stories that accompany your nervous system states. The elements of safety and connection build the foundation for your nervous system states and associated stories. Before turning the page, take the time to review the points that follow, and to engage in some simple activities to begin befriending your nervous system.

REFLECTING ON WHAT YOU'VE LEARNED

* Befriending your nervous system is an important process for reducing stress and avoiding feelings of being overwhelmed. Are you ready to befriend your nervous system? If not, what's holding you back?
* Your ANS has a hierarchy of predictable responses: ventral vagal, sympathetic, and dorsal vagal. Understanding how life looks from each of these states brings clarity, a fresh perspective, and an organized process for negotiating the hills and valleys we all experience in life. Begin simply by observing your states of response.
* Understanding that you and your students will go through different states throughout the day is a way of letting go of expectations of

being the perfect teacher in charge of the perfect classroom. Your classroom is a kaleidoscope of many different responses based on the nervous system states of each student. By keeping the ventral state in view, you teach your students how to do so as well. What small things can you do daily to help keep ventral energy flowing?

APPLYING WHAT YOU'VE LEARNED

Put what you've learned into action with the activities provided here to support you as you start your polyvagal journey. Choose a time when you can focus without interruption to complete the activities. Enjoy them on your own or with others if you are reading this with your book club, leadership team, friends, or family.

ACTIVITY ONE: Observing and Naming Your Nervous System States

When you observe and name your nervous system response states, you're better able to understand how you're feeling and what your nervous system needs in order to be regulated. The process goes like this: starting first thing in the morning, and as you move through your day, begin noticing and naming the states of your nervous system. Become familiar with the formal names of the states: ventral vagal, sympathetic, and dorsal vagal.

Once you're comfortable with the technical terms for the three states, use a bit of artistic license to personalize them by giving each a name that has meaning for you. For instance, you could associate your states with the weather: sunny for ventral vagal, stormy for sympathetic, and foggy for dorsal vagal. If you prefer, find objects that represent your states.

ACTIVITY TWO: Writing Autonomic Ladder Map Statements

Take a few moments to complete the following statements.

- I'm at the top of my Autonomic Ladder in a ventral vagal state when I . . .
- I begin to move down my Autonomic Ladder into a sympathetic state when I . . .
- I'm at the bottom of my Autonomic Ladder in a dorsal vagal state when I . . .

ACTIVITY THREE: Observing Students Through a Polyvagal Lens

With this new awareness of your nervous system states, begin observing students in your classroom. When you view their behavior through a polyvagal lens, you'll begin to recognize their nervous system response states. Start with observing and being curious. Where on the ladder does your nervous system go in response to your students' nervous systems? Don't try to solve anything or provide intervention (unless it's an urgent, unsafe situation, of course); if it's more of an annoyance than a safety issue, just observe.

CHAPTER 2

The Learning Foundation of Safety and Connection

We've all experienced, at one time or another, that sense of trepidation after typing an emotionally charged email and hitting the send button. For example, you've sent an email to a colleague that contains sensitive subject matter that may upset or anger the recipient. After hitting *send*, you doubt your decision. Unable to crawl through cyberspace to retrieve the email, your only option is to wait for a response. Anxious feelings begin within. Your chest tightens and your stomach knots. Days pass and still no response. The anxious feelings deepen. To make sense of your anxiety, your mind begins creating stories about your colleague being mad at you, disagreeing with you, or ignoring you.

Finally, after days stewing, the long-awaited response appears in your inbox. Within the lines of the email is an apology for taking so long to respond. A huge project with an impending deadline held up the response. Turns out, your colleague agrees with you and appreciated your candor. You sigh deeply, and the sense of uneasiness dissipates.

You've just experienced your mind as creative director, in charge of writing the scripts to go along with your nervous system states. Like any good author, your mind writes about what it knows. How does the mind create the

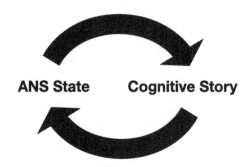

FIGURE 2.1   THE ANS STATE AND COGNITIVE STORY LOOP

elements of your stories? Let's use a process called Causal Layered Analysis (CLA) to explain (Inayatullah, 2017). Though the name makes the process sound difficult, it's an easily implemented framework that you'll find comes in handy when you continue befriending your nervous system. CLA helps you befriend your stories, commonly referred to as your narrative.

CLA is a predictable way of explaining how we create our narratives and how narratives change when presented with new information. The nervous system and the mind create a loop, with one affecting the other in a bidirectional, interactive conversation, continuously changing and evolving as nervous system states and stories interact with one another. Let's call this the ANS State and Cognitive Story Loop (Figure 2.1).

To bring CLA alive and understand how the loop works, let's visit a training where staff members' nervous system states and narratives so overshadowed the first hour that I had to stop the training to discover the deeper issues.

Causal Layered Analysis and Our Narratives

While leading a training for the special education department staff of a large school district in the Pacific Northwest, I noticed a lack of engagement from attendees. Most were on their phones or laptops. The few that were looking at me appeared unhappy and disinterested. I'd grown accustomed to mandated trainings being received with lukewarm enthusiasm by some staff members, but this time I sensed something bigger than the usual pushback brewing.

An hour into the presentation, I stopped and simply asked, "What's going on?" The floodgates opened, releasing a turbulent river of frustrations and concerns. Evidently, their department had hired a new special education director every year for the previous seven years, with each director doing a one-eighty in terms of policy and procedures.

Sensing a dysregulated group with nervous systems in either fight-or-flight mode or dorsal vagal despair, we needed to build a bridge to connection and find our way back to the top of our Autonomic Ladders. I needed to understand the narratives accompanying their nervous system states.

Using large sheets of paper and markers, the staff completed a CLA activity designed to organize and understand their narratives. I'd used this framework during hundreds of trainings, netting predictable, reliable, and valid outcomes each time—increased understanding among staff members and enhanced collaboration. With fingers crossed, I hoped to see similar, positive outcomes with this group.

CLA provides an organized process for articulating experiences, verbalizing concerns, uncovering barriers to positive change, and discovering scenarios that may create a space for transforming the narratives of individuals or a group (Inayatullah, 2017). The benefits for using CLA were:

- Ensuring all individual on the staff had an opportunity to describe their experiences and concerns arising from their staff positions.
- Uncovering factors and variables that contributed to the staff narratives.
- Identifying similarities and differences between individual narratives.
- Allowing for the safe expression of a range of scenarios and experiences.
- Organizing comments into a framework for easy sharing between individuals and groups.
- Ultimately, answering the question "What was holding back staff from engaging with me, connecting with one another, and achieving the objectives of the training?"

Using CLA enabled me to get up to speed quickly with the various concerns and challenges in the workplace. The litany layer provided the overview staff narrative of feeling unheard, unappreciated, unsupported, and

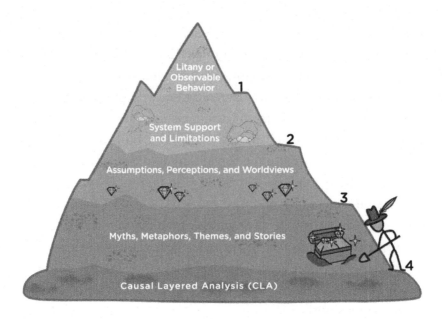

FIGURE 2.2   CLA LAYERS (drawn by Daniel S. Heiberger)

overworked. The second layer provided specific insights as to how the staff viewed system supports or limitations. The third layer unpacked personal assumptions and worldviews contributing to the narrative. The deepest layer uncovered myths and metaphors that the staff frequently repeated or used to describe how they felt about their workplace experiences.

It's important to note that the notion of causality is empirically problematic in the social sciences. This doesn't detract from the effectiveness of CLA as a practical framework. The objective of the facilitated process wasn't to determine a particular cause for the narratives but to explore multidimensional elements that staff attributed to each layer, thus informing the development of the subjective narrative. Working through the process made it possible to engage in rich discussions and gain fresh insights to collaboratively envision alternative and preferred futures (Inayatullah, 2017). Using CLA made it possible for the staff to envision a path to a less stressful and more enjoyable school year. Through completing the CLA activity, nervous system states and narratives shifted—more hopeful alternatives emerged.

Using the image of a mountain to demonstrate the layering process, we'll now dig into the layers and uncover how this specific staff had created their personal narratives (Figure 2.2). Put on your explorer hat, and we'll go through the CLA process.

The first step in CLA is to examine what we see on the surface of the mountain. This is the litany or observable behavior layer—the account of events expressed through day-to-day conversations, mainstream media headlines, and data reporting. The standard, widely held, or superficial understanding of the issue makes up the first layer (Voros, 2005). In our professional training, school staff shared elements of the first layer:

- concerns about being blamed for data showing limited gains for students
- uncertainty about how to gather data on students as the process constantly changes
- uncertainty about what are considered effective gains for students
- fear of looming lawsuits from unhappy parents
- wondering about the motives of the new director
- fretting about what changes were in the works

Having discussed and written down their top-layer responses, the groups moved into the systems layer.

In the second layer, we unearthed the rocks and sediment that sit underneath the topsoil. At the systems layer, the question becomes, "How do the organization and systems in place support or limit the observable behaviors?" The staff listed ways they felt supported or unsupported by their administration, general education staff, and families. Only a few items appeared on the support lists. The unsupported lists included:

- uncertainty about paperwork protocol
- scheduling challenges
- inadequate training in the new curriculum adoptions
- unclear assessment procedures
- not enough time to collaborate
- parents failing to show up for meetings
- limited funding to meet their students' needs

In the third layer, the group focus shifted from the factors outside of the individual to the inner world of assumptions, perceptions, and worldviews. The staff dug deep into beliefs formed through their personal histories, biases, and experiences. In this layer, they discovered diamonds—precious gemstones that are known for their hardness—and just like personal beliefs, they resist scratching, chipping, or changing. The staff uncovered their buried diamonds one by one:

- It's impossible to meet all the differing stakeholder needs.
- Teachers are unwilling to collaborate and do not want staff in their rooms.
- The staff's opinions don't matter.
- The organization is irreparable, and the problems are too big to fix.

The fourth layer is where the staff began to unearth their deeply buried treasure chests of myths, metaphors, themes, and deeply held stories. It's at this deepest layer that they opened these chests and discovered sparkling gems of constructed reality—forged out of pressure, tension, generations of recurring themes, and repeated cultural stories. Metaphors (or common expressions) shed light on the staff's deepest issues.

- The right hand doesn't know what the left hand is doing.
- It's like pushing water uphill.
- I'm just a cog in a wheel.
- Data rules the day.

The myths included, "The administration is a bunch of data collectors," "They don't care about how hard we work," and "Nothing ever changes in education, so why bother?"

Where Transformation Begins

As the staff worked through the activity and deconstructed their layers of understanding, discussions led to empowering insights, and ventral energy came back into the room. The staff felt safe engaging with me—I was no longer the enemy, the person taking up their valuable time with an unwelcomed seminar.

Together, we completed the reconstructing portion of CLA, this time working from the deepest layers up to the top layer. I asked, "What changes can you make today to create the future you want tomorrow?" With new insights gained from deconstructing their issues, the myth of the uncaring administration was replaced with an understanding that everyone, including administrators, seemed overwhelmed. The theme of "we don't matter" became "we all matter, so how can we support one another?" More hopeful metaphors emerged:

- It takes a village.
- Be the change you want to see.
- Take one step at a time.
- Together we're stronger.

Within the context of more optimistic metaphors, the staff revisited their former assumptions, perceptions, and worldviews while moving up into the third layer of the CLA process. Viewing administration as uncaring shifted to the realization that a shortage of personnel required individuals to wear multiple hats, burdening them with additional responsibility. The belief that teachers were unwilling to collaborate morphed into understanding that they didn't have time to collaborate due to new curriculum adoptions and uncertainty about assessment procedures. The staff's assumptions, perceptions, and worldviews then became:

- The teachers want what's best for students, including our support.
- Collaboration is a key to improving our job satisfaction.
- Students can meet their goals if we work together.
- There's an opportunity for growth and change.

Taking the staff's newly found optimism into the second or systems layer, a consensus formed between individuals and groups, making it possible to see system strengths while also discovering ways to ask for more support, including:

- sharing successful strategies with one another
- vocalizing their desires to connect with monthly meetings
- a commitment to continue working through the challenges together
- asking their director to read the CLA summaries they created to bring awareness to staff needs

With laptops closed, phones down, smiles returning to their faces, and body language relaxing, a space opened that allowed for the possibility of transformational change—creating a brighter future. Through the safety of CLA and connecting with one another, the staff settled into a focused day of learning, embracing their time in the training with renewed enthusiasm at the prospect of gaining valuable strategies to enhance future collaboration.

> ## PRINCIPLE TWO: Safety and connection lead to motivation and engagement.

This principle holds true for both staff attending trainings and students learning in the classroom. The director, not present during the training, received positive comments from the staff during the lunch break and at the end of the training. Curious, he asked to discuss the results of the CLA activity with me. While sitting down together and reading comments from each of the groups, I heard an audible sigh, observed his shoulders relaxing, and sensed a true willingness to listen and connect with the staff—creating a transformative space for change.

Using CLA provides deeper insights into the ANS States and Cognitive Story Loop. The framework is an excellent addition to your toolbox and can be used during staff meeting discussions, professional trainings, or class with students to provide a safe, organized method for discussing complex topics and issues.

The Three Cs of Safety: Choice, Context, and Connection

The staff's nervous system states and narratives contributed to the initial rough start to the training. However, additional elements affected the disconnection between the staff and myself—explained through the polyvagal concepts of safety and connection.

In this staff development experience, the group initially resisted engaging with me because the Three Cs of Safety were missing—choice, context, and connection (Dana, 2018). The staff didn't have a choice about attending the training, nor had the director asked their opinions about the professional development priorities for the year. With choice comes a sense of control. They had no control over the mandated training.

In addition, holding the training during the first week of school created more stress for a staff already bombarded by the beginning-of-the-year frenzy, including emails and questions from parents and teachers. Within the context of a new school year, the staff needed the first week to respond to questions, get schedules sorted out, and find their bearings. A training tossed into the middle of this week only added more static to their already frayed nervous systems.

Finally, the staff lacked a sense of connection. It's the connection within relationships that provides perceptions of safety. When sensing danger within, the ability to reach out to others for support and comfort is essential if the nervous system is to feel safe. From the administration to the staff members, most appeared to be going it alone with little to no support from one another.

The Signals of Safety and Danger

Our autonomic nervous systems are continuously scanning the environment, checking out people and situations to make sure everything's on the up and up. This scanning process is always running in the background, but we're unaware of it. Dr. Porges (2017) coined the term *neuroception* to describe how the ANS is on call 24/7 to ensure that it's safe for us to engage.

If we bring perception to neuroception, we then consciously identify the sense of safety and danger. To regulate our nervous systems, we must increase feelings of safety and reduce feelings of danger. It's like balancing a nervous system math equation.

Think of an old-fashioned scale with the signals of danger on one end, and on the other end, signals of safety (Figure 2.3). When signals of

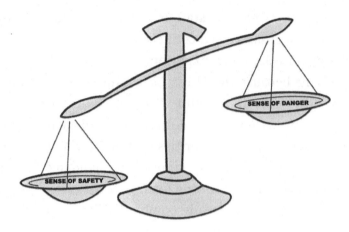

FIGURE 2.3   THE SAFETY SCALE (drawn by Daniel S. Heiberger)

danger are present, more signals of safety are needed to balance the scale (Dana, 2018). Not all items have equal weight. At times there may be only one item on the danger side of the scale, but it's something that feels very unsafe and carries a lot of weight.

Feelings of safety and danger come from inside us, outside in the environment, and between people in relationships (Dana, 2018).

Signals From Inside

We bring perception to neuroception through interoceptive awareness—the ability to consciously feel the internal state of the body (Mahler, 2017). Feeling hungry, needing to go to the bathroom, feeling your heart beating fast, or sensing the tension of stress in your muscles are examples of being in touch with your internal bodily states.

Improving interoceptive awareness is a meaningful objective for all of us. Honing one's interoceptive sense aligns with good judgment, making better decisions, acting less impulsively, planning, and dealing with others who might make us feel uncomfortable (Paul, 2021).

Biological rudeness is a term used to explain how our nervous systems respond in those moments when people walk away, look down at their phones, or ignore us in some way (Porges, 2017). Biological rudeness evokes an uncomfortable visceral response deep within us. We're better able to acknowledge, understand, and respond to the effects of biological rudeness on our nervous systems when we have good interoceptive awareness. Recognizing information coming from inside our bodies is essential for processing information from outside in the environment.

Signals From Outside

Look around and notice where you are right now. If you're at home in your own personal space reading this book, there's a good chance you're feeling safe and your ANS is humming along in the background, allowing you to read and remember this information without sending you warning signs about imminent danger.

On the other hand, if you're reading this book at dusk in a park where people are packing up and going home, your nervous system might be sensing that you're heading into dangerous territory—being alone in the park after dark. These nudges of danger make it harder for you to focus, continue reading, and comprehend the text. Your need to head home to safety is greater than your need to remain in the park and read.

Feelings of safety and danger are variables for people. What one person senses as safe may be unsafe to another based on individual histories. A few ideas for increasing a sense of safety generally for everyone in the classroom include:

- rules, procedures, and schedules clearly explained and posted with visuals to accompany words
- preparation in advance for fire drills, substitutes, and unexpected events
- options to learn in a variety of ways that feel good to the nervous system, with spaces designed for quiet alone time, partner work, or active learning through movement

Though it's impossible to ensure everyone in class always feels safe, starting with a baseline of implementable strategies provides an entry point for nurturing most nervous systems in the classroom environment.

Signals Between Ourselves and Others

The Social Engagement System is the system of connection that is active when we are in a ventral vagal state (Porges, 2021). This system is also called the face-heart connection created by the vagus pathway from the heart to the face. Open-hearted connection is expressed through the welcoming look in the eyes, the crinkle around the eyes when smiling, attentive body language, willingness to listen, and tone of voice. The face-heart connection is present during typical births, with bidirectional neural communication between mother and child in the form of the suck-swallow-breathe-vocalize synchrony—the core of the Social Engagement System (Porges, 2017).

Through this system, we watch for welcoming or warning signs in people we encounter through the course of the day. Sometimes we don't know why we sense danger from a person. It's usually in their face, tone of voice, or certain ways they move. If something is too intense or feels out of place, it's probably a cue of danger from the past. It's implicit first and made explicit when you become aware of the discomfort coming from within you through interoception. When this happens, ask yourself, "In this moment, in this place, with this person, is this response necessary?" This brings awareness to the process of neuroception. As soon as you recognize that you don't need to protect yourself in this situation with this person, you can bring more ventral energy to the experience.

When the Social Engagement System is in operation, it allows you to connect with others and fills the need we all have to be seen and heard—knowing someone is listening to understand, rather than listening only to respond. This perception of safety allows us to move toward another person—physically and emotionally.

The Social Engagement System plays a role in the ability of students and staff to relate to one another through understanding the positive impact of a calm voice, welcoming soft eye gaze, friendly demeanor, and open body language poised to listen.

The Safety–Academic Link

A growing body of research suggests that the safer and more connected to one another staff members feel, the better students perform academically.

In a mixed-methods study focusing on collaboration between occupational therapists and general education teachers, key themes emerged aligning with the Three Cs of Safety, including collaboration as a choice, feeling safe to take risks within the context of working together in classrooms, and a sense of connection and friendship with one another (Wilson, 2015).

The partner teams collaborated and created environments where the signals of safety outnumbered the signals of danger—providing nourishment for their nervous systems and a safe place for them and their students to work together. The positive collaborative relationships ultimately increased the number of students meeting their academic goals.

A safe school environment is a prerequisite for productive learning. According to a three-year study of 340,000 New York City middle school students and 700 middle schools, students who feel safe are more focused and engaged. Feeling unsafe in classrooms significantly correlated with lower test scores (Lacoe, 2020).

In a National Public Radio report, students from Baltimore City public schools walked to school or used the public bus system because no school buses were provided through the school system. Researchers from Johns Hopkins University mapped the routes high school freshmen traveled to and from school. Many students walked several blocks out of their way or transferred to different buses to avoid dangerous neighborhoods, adding time to their already long commute. Given the difficulty of getting to school, 37% of students from higher-crime neighborhoods were chronically absent (Nadworny, 2019). When students risk navigating a dangerous route, imagine the state of their nervous systems upon arrival at school. Applying the Three Cs of Safety can support their nervous systems and help with attention and engagement.

Safety Through Choices

Each student's nervous system may need different forms of nourishment, so allow some autonomic choices. To maximize the benefits, offer students a limited number of options. Too many choices may cause confusion and lead to decreased motivation. Somewhere between three to five choices is the sweet spot, according to a meta-analysis study focusing on intrinsic motivation (Patall et al., 2008). As the adage goes, "A confused mind always says no." There *can* be too much of a good thing.

An example of three choices before beginning academics might be:

1. Sitting quietly and listening to pleasing music for five minutes with an option to draw or do something artistic.
2. Watching a nature video for a few minutes.
3. Participating in an enjoyable rhythmic group activity.

Safety Through Context

Along with providing choice, create context. According to the *Oxford English Dictionary*, context refers to the circumstances that make a situation, idea, or words understandable or meaningful. For example, consider the words on a message inside a fortune cookie: "Your life path will be rocky but rewarding in the end." To most people reading the fortune, the words express a sense of foreboding that life is going to be tough, painful, and unpleasant until a particular milestone is reached. However, if you're an off-roading enthusiast who owns a vehicle set up for climbing rocks, this fortune is perfect! What off-roader doesn't like a rocky path with a rewarding end—say, looking out over Arches National Park after completing the black diamond course? The way we interpret and understand information has everything to do with context.

For all students (especially those who have traveled a difficult path just to show up for school), providing good reasons for attendance is paramount. Providing context is an essential brain-based and nervous-system-friendly strategy. Though the metaphor for the brain is often a computer, we're much more like animals than machines, and yet the myth prevails. The human brain is very different from a computer—it's exquisitely sensitive to context (Paul, 2021). As teachers, being context creators is an essential part of our jobs. It's what's going on outside the brain that forms connections inside the brain.

Examples of providing context include:

- showing how students use what they're learning outside the classroom
- designing engaging environments that grab students' attention
- inviting students to participate in measuring outcomes for projects

- encouraging learners to personalize assignments so they are meaningful and relevant to their lives

Evidence supports a correlation between assessment outcomes and students' experiences related to context. Two decades of research on grades 6–12 reading intervention classes in the United States has validated the relationship between context and learning. Data related to students' experiences and perspectives found improved outcomes when students viewed coursework as relevant and personally meaningful (Frankel et al., 2021).

Safety Through Connection

When choice and context meet with connection, the formula for safety unfolds and the stage is set for optimized learning. Trauma, however, whether it be shock (isolated event) or developmental (ongoing abuse, neglect, or manipulation in early childhood), compromises a student's ability to engage with others by replacing patterns of connection with patterns of protection (Kain & Terrell, 2018). In all types of trauma, automatic protective responses are actions intended to help you survive—just like a car alarm going off without a real threat.

Remember that viewing classroom situations through a polyvagal lens allows educators to offer opportunities for students' nervous systems to increase flexibility by learning how to engage, disengage, and reengage.

Providing enough safety and offering enough connection to meet the student where their nervous system is in the present moment is a good path forward. However, keep in mind that your invitation to connect with a student may not be received immediately. Think of a turtle in a shell. You wouldn't shake it or knock on the shell to hurry along the turtle's process of coming out into the world. You would wait patiently, and in due time with the right amount of safety, the turtle appears. It may be next year's teacher who sees the turtle fully emerge; however, you've extended the lettuce leaf of encouragement and connection.

Loneliness and Its Impact on Academic Achievement

The opposite of connection is loneliness. Despite our best efforts to help students build relationships and form supportive connections with peers at school, some remain like the turtle—looking out from inside a shell, unable, for whatever reasons, to form friendships. Dr. Vivek Murthy, U.S. surgeon general and author of the insightful book, *Together*, describes it as

> *the subjective feeling that you're lacking the social connections you need. It can feel like being stranded, abandoned, or cut off from the people with whom you belong—even if you're surrounded by other people. What's missing when you're lonely is the feeling of closeness, trust, and the affection of genuine friends, loved ones, and community.* (2020, p. 8)

Loneliness differs from solitude. Solitude is something chosen, savored, or spiritually desired. Introverts tend to seek more solitude than extroverts (Cain, 2013). In solitude, there is connection, not necessarily to others in the moment but to oneself. Solitude has an element of joy in being alone. Loneliness, on the other hand, is uncomfortable and not something freely chosen or enjoyed.

Loneliness may look like depression, anxiety, aloofness, indifference, or anger. In fact, research findings show that loneliness is one of the main antecedents for smartphone addiction that leads to poor academic performance (Mahapatra, 2019). Loneliness reduces a student's ability to focus and engage, negatively impacting academic success (Benner, 2011). Students reported more academic burnout, stress, and less ability to cope in the classroom when experiencing loneliness (Stolinker & Lafreniere, 2015).

Moreover, students who experience loneliness can be in a self-perpetuating cycle of shame about not being able to make friends easily. This can lower self-esteem, further reducing the confidence to reach out and attempt to make friends and increasing the chances of being targeted for bullying.

One of the saddest memories I have of my daughter in school is a day when I stopped in unexpectedly. I observed children on the playground laughing, chasing one another, swinging, going down slides—and there in the corner of the blacktop stood Shalea—all alone, isolated at the edge of a crowd. I got out of my car, walked over to her, and took her into my arms, wiping her tears away while I fought to hold mine at bay. The recess bell rang and together we walked back to class. There's a little place in my heart where that memory of loneliness resides.

Stepping Onto the Joyful Path to Learning

Polyvagal Theory provides a biological explanation for the importance of developing relationships. We are wired for connection from birth through adulthood (Porges, 2021). Safe and supportive relationships bring beauty and meaning to our lives, and a consistent reminder that we're not alone.

When feeling lonely and disconnected from others, it's important to cultivate what researchers call the three dimensions of relationships—intimate, relational, and collective (Murthy, 2020).

- Intimate relationships are formed with our closest family members.
- Relational refers to our quality friendships or peer bonds that provide support at home, work, or play.
- Collective relationships are networks we develop through communities, such as church or special interest groups.

As educators, one of the most effective ways we can help reduce loneliness in the classroom or on the playground is to help students become a part of a group that's meeting a need on campus. When in service to others, they can often find the connections and friendships they've been missing.

Although many variables determine a student's level of engagement and attention, the recurrent variable in research studies is the student's sense of safety (Sparks, 2013; Côté-Lussier & Fitzpatrick, 2016). The ability to pay attention is generally perceived as a cognitive experience requiring the right mix of brain chemicals and frontal lobe activation, but it's also a whole-body and sensing experience, in which safety and connection play an important role.

Now let's take all you've learned about befriending your nervous system, unpacking cognitive stories, and the relationship between safety and connection into Chapter 3, where we'll view the concept of regulation through a polyvagal lens.

REFLECTING ON WHAT YOU'VE LEARNED

- Dr. Porges states that safety is the treatment in therapy. Do you think safety is also an important intervention in the classroom? Why or why not?

- CLA is a process for understanding how we create cognitive stories. With it we can deconstruct our stories and discover the deeper layers moving from the external world to our internal worlds. As you learn to befriend your nervous system, use the ANS State and Cognitive Story Loop to observe how your ANS states and stories affect one another. Can you think of an example of this loop playing out in a recent experience?

- The Three Cs of Safety are choice, context, and connection. Think of two situations in your classroom: one that went well and one that didn't go well. Did the elements of choice, context, and connection make a difference in the outcomes?

- Relationships include three dimensions: intimate, relational, and collective. Do you have relational resources at school that provide support when you're feeling lonely or disconnected in your job? How can our schools create opportunities for students to develop their three relationship dimensions?

APPLYING WHAT YOU'VE LEARNED

ACTIVITY ONE: Experiencing the ANS State and Cognitive Story Loop

Bring awareness to your nervous system states and your thinking process. Consider a situation right now that makes you feel as if you're stuck without being able to discover a way forward. Check in. Can you name the state of your nervous system? Are you also able to notice the stories your mind is creating? How is your ANS State and Cognitive Story Loop supporting or limiting you in this situation?

ACTIVITY TWO: Exploring CLA for Understanding Two Viewpoints

Choose a controversial topic that keeps coming up at school, home, or in the media. Using the CLA process, compare two opposing viewpoints by exploring each of the four layers. Is there more potential for open communication after going through the layering process? Checking in with your nervous system states while going through the process adds an additional perspective. Observe and name your states as you explore your stories while being aware of the positive impact keeping one foot in a ventral vagal state may bring to provide additional insights.

ACTIVITY THREE: Observing Signals of Safety and Danger

Choose one student at school who tends to have a challenging day four days out of five. Observe the student through the lens of safety and connection. How many aspects of safety and danger can you uncover for that student? Is there a way to provide more signals of safety than danger by bringing awareness to feelings of safety from inside the body, outside in the environment, and between others?

ACTIVITY FOUR: Creating a Project to Remedy Loneliness

Have you noticed any staff members or students in your school who appear lonely? Create a project that fills a school or community need and invite those individuals to participate.

CHAPTER 3

Regulation Through a Polyvagal Lens

You're well on your way to understanding how to befriend your nervous system and the important role of safety and connection in optimizing learning. Let's continue your polyvagal journey by heading over to Green Acres, a little out-of-the-way portable classroom—a sanctuary for high school students lacking support from home and struggling to meet the academic requirements to graduate. It's here at Green Acres where an event transpires that serves as a powerful example of how quickly things in the classroom can spiral out of control when nervous systems jump off their regulated, ventral path.

A Sympathetic Storm

When I discovered nearly half my high school biology students couldn't read their texts well enough to understand key concepts, I returned to school to earn a master's degree in education along with a reading specialist credential.

In the second year of my master's program and eager to use newly acquired clinical reading skills, I moved from teaching biology to teaching high school students who, for a variety of reasons, were in independent study programs and at risk of dropping out of school. I affectionately called the portable where I taught Green Acres, a tattered and torn lonely building on a remote back acre off a deserted country road few people knew existed.

For my master's project, I created a reading intervention program for high school students. The aims of the program were to improve students' attitudes toward reading, decrease learned helplessness, increase meta-cognitive strategies, and use evidence-based reading techniques to hone literacy skills.

Mr. Parker, the principal from the alternative high school, selected 12 ninth-grade boys to attend the program three hours per day during the spring quarter. The students read below the third grade level, experienced challenging home situations, and participated in gang activity in the community.

Knowing these boys were going to schlep their backpacks full of trauma and resentment of authority into my classroom, I needed the students to view me as an ally and not the enemy. I visited the main high school campus and asked for 12 driver's education textbooks (a subject still taught at that time). Next, I drove to the local DMV to get written sample driving tests for each student. Prepared to engage them from the get-go, I handed each a test as they walked in the door for the first day of class. Knowing they couldn't read well enough to pass this test, I asked, "Would you like to get a driver's license someday?" All nodded in agreement. We rallied around a worthwhile goal.

The students came to class just about every day, motivated to improve their reading skills well enough to pass the driver's test. If they missed days, it was usually to nurse injuries from a weekend fight. One student pushed through the near-fatal wounds of his weekend, showing up with a bandage around his head and sharing with the group, "Oh, I was shot in a drive-by, but the bullet only grazed me." The dedication these teens showed in the face of adversity proved the power of connection and being seen—each day.

Come state standardized testing time, Principal Parker thought it best that the students take their tests with me at Green Acres because they trusted me. The students did a fantastic job with an entire week of testing. They focused. Chewed on pencils. Applied themselves. Maintained positive attitudes. Truly impressive.

When the last test was taken and test booklets closed, I asked the students what they'd like to do with the few minutes before class ended.

"Let's make paper airplanes and fly them around the room!" one said.

"Sure, why not?" I said. What bad thing could come of that?

Let me remind you we were hanging out in Green Acres, a place where no one from administration ever visited, except for Principal Parker—occasionally. Pleasant, supportive, and complimentary, Principal Parker's visits always left me confident that I was handling my teaching responsibilities with some aplomb. Little did I know that same morning of final test completion, Principal Parker had shared the success I'd been having with the students with the head of the school board, whom we'll call Dr. Smith, who had a doctorate in education. Curious, Dr. Smith, whom I'd never met, decided to stroll on over and have a look for himself. He walked up the ramp, opened the door, and we became acquainted as a paper airplane grazed his ear.

He took in the scene for a moment and with clenched fists shouted these spittle-chased words, "Consider yourself fired! You'll never teach another day in any school system."

Growing up with domestic violence, my nervous system is always on high alert for a man who's about to lose or has lost his temper. Dr. Smith's reaction activated a nervous system response based on events from my past. Speechless and stunned, I stood there trying to make myself invisible; my students low in their seats, all of us were holding our collective breath. He stormed out—his cloud-filled nervous system of turbulence following behind him, leaving us all in a state of shock. Trying to save what little dignity I had left, I dismissed the students and sat dazed in my chair (with visions of unpaid student loans dancing in my head).

In defense of Dr. Smith, walking into a classroom as airplanes sail past one's head does evoke teacher incompetence. Consequently, his nervous system activated an immediate sympathetic response. This was not altogether an inappropriate response considering that a classroom with students out of control is a dangerous situation. His nervous system, however, misjudged the level of threat.

Celebrating test completion with paper airplanes, the students and I were humming along in ventral vagal and sharing the connection and affection we felt for one another. Dr. Smith's dysregulated nervous system caused our nervous systems to tumble down the rungs of the ladder, landing us at the bottom. Meanwhile, Dr. Smith's nervous system firmly clung to the middle rungs of his automatic ladder—fight! At this point, there were no adults in the room with regulated nervous systems. We were in the midst of a sympathetic storm with no umbrella to shield us from the freezing hail.

In Principal Parker's office, Dr. Smith described what he'd witnessed—a management-challenged teacher with out-of-control students. Still in a sympathetic state, he insisted Principal Parker fire me. Remember, you can't be sympathetic in sympathetic!

After Dr. Smith had left the school, Principal Parker skedaddled over to Green Acres. Opening the door and entering the crime scene, he pulled up a chair and sat beside me. His warm smile reached all the way up to the crinkle around his eyes, creating a feeling of safety that helped bring my Social Engagement System back online. As he shared his regulated nervous system with me, I gathered my thoughts and frazzled nervous system, and the story unfolded. Through co-regulation, I tapped into Principal Parker's ventral energy and moved up my own Autonomic Ladder. Together and from a ventral vagal state, we viewed the options and created a plan to correct the misunderstanding and keep me dutifully employed.

Borrowers and Lenders

In Shakespeare's play, *Hamlet*, Polonius gives Laertes advice on money with his famous trope, "neither a borrower nor a lender be." While this may be useful for money, it's poor advice for our nervous systems.

One of the most hopeful perspectives of Polyvagal Theory is the notion that we can reach out to another and borrow their regulated nervous system or loan our regulated nervous system to someone else. Through borrowing and loaning, we create opportunities to co-regulate with one another.

Co-regulation is a biological imperative and developmentally comes before self-regulation (Porges, 2017). We enter the world needing co-regulation with other humans. To survive, the nervous system looks for safe relationships with others.

Think of the mother and child relationship in which the nervous system of each is affected by the other, leading to co-regulation or co-dysregulation (Badenoch, 2018). When mom successfully makes baby smile, the two are co-regulating—activating the Social Engagement System. If baby then becomes dysregulated, mom may become dysregulated as well. The third principle of Polyvagal Theory emphasizes the biological priority of co-regulation—and that's often overlooked when educators focus on self-regulation.

PRINCIPLE THREE: Co-regulation comes before self-regulation.

As children grow in healthy family relationships, their capacities for self-regulation increase; however, the need for co-regulation remains. We must experience enough safe co-regulation with people we trust before we can consistently self-regulate.

In classrooms, self-regulation is considered a learned skill essential for emotional, behavioral, and academic success. Self-regulation is defined as how well a person is able to modify and control their thoughts, feelings, and behaviors in order to meet goals or standards (Freund & Hennecke, 2015). A unique perspective of Polyvagal Theory is viewing self-regulation through the lens of safety. The theory defines self-regulation as the ability of the nervous system to "maintain feelings of safety in the absence of receiving cues of safety from another person" (Porges, 2017, p. 25).

If co-regulation isn't predictably available in a safe way (for an infant, child, or adult), we can learn how to self-regulate in order to survive, but it's draining rather than nourishing for the nervous system. Porges continues, "The theory emphasizes that the mutual, synchronous, and reciprocal interactions between individuals that define co-regulation function as a neural exercise enhancing the ability to self-regulate in the absence of opportunities to co-regulate" (p. 25).

In the absence of opportunities to safely co-regulate, other behaviors may surface when a child is forced to self-regulate but the nervous system hasn't had the safe, priming co-regulating experiences that make self-regulation possible.

As we co-regulate with learners, we help them understand their nervous systems by modeling the naming of our own nervous system states. By literally asking aloud, "What does my nervous system need right now?" you are teaching learners how to ask themselves what their own nervous systems need to be regulated. Depending on the day or situation, your students' systems may require different amounts of co-regulation with another person.

If a student is having difficulty with self-regulation, offer co-regulating experiences rather than continuing to expect self-regulation. For instance, you could ask a second student to sit next to the one needing support with regulation. Together they could work on an assignment, do a partner movement activity, or take turns reading to one another. It's through co-regulation that students learn to notice, name, and focus on their own nervous system states, rather than focusing on the event going on in real time. Providing easily accessible regulating resources restores ventral energy when it's going offline.

Remember the ANS State and Cognitive Story Loop discussed earlier? As the state changes, the cognitive story changes. If you and your students can learn how to observe and name your states before talking about the story or incident, you may find that the narrative changes. The way students respond in situations is no longer a mystery, and they gain more control, honing their abilities to understand their nervous system states. They're more able to discover what regulating resources are needed in the moment either from within themselves or through co-regulation with another person. Students move from helplessness into empowerment when they're able to tap into resources outside themselves as well as from within. The shift from focusing on self-regulation to understanding the importance of co-regulation challenges a common assumption of many programs—that self-regulation is the goal.

Interactive Regulation

When the focus is on self-regulation, we limit the resources available to lighten the regulatory load. Dr. Bonnie Badenoch (2018), author of *The*

Heart of Trauma, posits that we truly never regulate by ourselves. Using the term *interactive regulation* is a way to understand regulation as an ongoing interaction between our nervous systems and the resources we carry within us, the people who offer safe reciprocating and co-regulating experiences, and the sense of safety from the environment.

We are always regulating interactively with a variety of interconnected resources. Classrooms are communities of nervous systems influencing the states of others. It's in the balance of the borrowing and lending of nervous systems that ventral energy becomes a resource available if students know how to find it in one another.

The ultimate destination in most regulation programs is self-regulation. Polyvagal Theory explains why it may be the journey with others rather than the destination alone that nourishes the nervous system and provides regulatory resources that are difficult to tap into on one's own.

The View from Ventral

A helpful way to understand the autonomic nervous system is to view events from different nervous system states. Focus on events that aren't traumatic but part of the day-to-day interactions with others—the small stuff. Doing so increases your understanding of events through different lenses and allows you to see possible options. For example, let's return to the sympathetic storm at Green Acres and retell the story using a ventral vagal point of view. Though nudging more toward the traumatic end of the scale at the time, it's an experience I can easily view with ventral energy now.

• • •

Dr. Smith walks into my classroom, naturally a bit shocked (and heading toward sympathetic activation); but he manages to stay in ventral vagal.

He takes in the disappointing display of apparent classroom mismanagement, and pulling me aside, calmly asks, "Can you tell me what's going on right now?"

Embarrassed at the timing of his visit, I say, "My students have been *model* test-takers all week. They've focused and attempted to answer all the questions. With the last test complete, I asked them what they'd like to do for the remaining fifteen minutes of class, and they wanted to make paper airplanes."

Dr. Smith's surprise visit holds the potential of sending us down our ladders, but due to his composure, we stay at the top and my students observe an adult who handles himself in a way that teaches them how to manage a situation with calmness and curiosity rather than with quick judgment and assumptions.

Turning to the class, he says, "Wow, I heard you did a great job with your testing this week. How do you feel about showing up for testing and doing your best?" My students reply, "The tests were hard, but we did our best. We're glad they're over!"

Dr. Smith picks up one of the wayward airplanes, analyzes the dynamic properties of flight, decides to make one himself, and flies it towards the students. The plane lifts for a nanosecond and then hits the floor with a thud. We all laugh together—feeling safe, connected, and co-regulating with one another.

Imagining how an event could have transpired while in a ventral vagal state is good practice and sets the foundation for better outcomes when a similar situation arises in the future.

The Regulated Learner

Given that Polyvagal Theory defines self-regulation and co-regulation as they relate to nervous system states and you're familiar with the concept of regulation coming from a variety of ventral resources—how does this relate to years of research on self-regulated learning, co-regulated learning, and socially shared regulated learning?

Let's start by understanding how education researchers define these three terms, as their viewpoint differs from those using a polyvagal lens. Primarily, education researchers address where the regulating sources come from as they meet goals, monitor progress, and adjust strategies as needed (Figure 3.1).

Type of Learning	Source of Regulation
● Self-regulated Learning	Inside the learner, relying on self
●● Co-regulated Learning	Outside the learner, relying on a teacher, mentor, tutor, or more knowledgeable peer
✿ Socially Shared Learning	Between a group of learners, relying on one another

FIGURE 3.1: THE SOURCE OF REGULATION FOR THREE TYPES OF LEARNING

Self-Regulated Learning

Self-regulated learning refers to "how learners set goals and then systematically employ procedures that support goal achievement" (Andrade et al., 2021, p. 3). Zimmerman (1990) describes self-regulated learners as "metacognitively, motivationally, and behaviorally active participants in their own learning" (p. 4).

Self-regulated learning emphasizes the active role of the student in accomplishing learning objectives and self-monitoring progress toward meeting specific goals through self-reported regulation of learning proficiency (Bransen et al., 2021). Self-regulated learners are aware of task requirements and their own needs regarding optimization of their academic learning. They actively use cognitive strategies and view learning as a process within their control through utilizing strategies to plan, organize, monitor, and evaluate their path to goal attainment or task completion (Mega et al., 2014).

Models of self-regulated learning vary and generally follow or elaborate on four stages to describe a regulated learning episode. A learning episode includes time periods before, during, and after task completion. According to Andrade et al. (2021), the four stages are:

1. Phase 1: forethought, planning, and activation
2. Phase 2: monitoring of motivation and cognitive strategies

3. Phase 3: selection and adaptation of cognitive strategies for learning and thinking

4. Phase 4: reaction, reflection, evaluation of task

A self-regulated learner completes these stages independently and is cued into their motivation levels, thoughts related to how things are going, and the need for revising strategies that may not be working (metacognition). They know how to find and apply cognitive resources from inside themselves as needed to complete academic tasks.

Co-regulated Learning

Co-regulated learning is typically described as a process where the regulation of learning is guided by someone more capable, usually a teacher, mentor, tutor, or peer. This learner relies on a co-regulating person, in the learner's environment, to monitor and mediate the metacognitive and cognitive processes of an individual or group. Learners rely on support from outside themselves rather than using inner resources. Feedback is provided by the leader and guides students through the process of monitoring learning, utilizing effective strategies, and reflecting on learning as a transition to self-regulated learning (Hadwin & Oshige, 2011).

In self-regulated and co-regulated learning models, learning is more of a thinking experience and not as much of a feeling experience. Nervous system states and associated cognitive stories are not integrated into the academic models.

Socially Shared Regulation of Learning

With the limitations of self-regulated learning and co-regulated learning models, the term *socially shared regulation of learning* entered learning model research and designs. Through collaborative and team-based learning, regulation of learning becomes a collective, reciprocal, evenly distributed, and shared experience between learners focusing on completion of tasks based on collective monitoring of goal progression (Bransen et al., 2021).

The fact that all three regulation models focus primarily on cognitive skills created a gap between research focusing on the role of emotions in learning and the cognitive processes involved in goal attainment.

Researchers Mega et al. (2014) introduced a theoretical model linking emotions, self-regulated learning, and motivation to academic achievement. The role of emotions in learning has been set aside in regulated learning models. However, we're now nudging ever closer to discovering ways to integrate Polyvagal Theory into current theoretical learning models.

Academic Emotional Learning

As a result, academic emotional learning refers to the role of emotions in affecting academic outcomes. These emotions are usually grounded in prior learning experiences. For instance, if a student's past experiences with math have been positive and enjoyable, the student's affective inclination toward participating in additional math activities most likely will initially be positive.

The phases of academic emotional learning describe how active learners monitor and adjust their emotions by using strategies called self-regulated emotion strategies (Figure 3.2; Ben-Eliyahu, 2019).

This learning cycle includes the *affective inclination* (how a student feels about learning a particular subject or completing a task) prior to the start of the learning episode. During the learning episode, the student monitors feelings (enjoyment, confidence, frustration, anger, stress, etc.). In the final phase of the cycle, students complete their learning episode and evaluate emotions focused on achievement (Ben-Eliyahu, 2019). It's important to explicitly teach regulation of emotions throughout the learning episode.

And this is the perfect place for integrating Polyvagal Theory into learning models. Optimally, learning happens when the learner is in a ventral vagal state—during which learning is not only a thinking experience but also a feeling experience. Our nervous systems carry ventral,

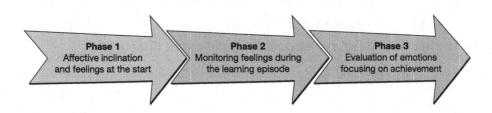

FIGURE 3.2   ACADEMIC EMOTIONAL LEARNING PHASES

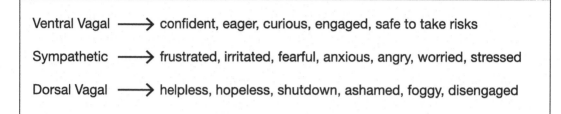

FIGURE 3.3   ANS STATES AND RELATED ACADEMIC EMOTIONS

sympathetic, and dorsal energy—all necessary responses depending on the situation—but we want ventral energy running in the foreground.

Viewing regulated learning through a polyvagal lens, academic emotions are related to specific nervous system states and dependent upon the foundations of safety and connection (Figure 3.3).

Observing and shifting states during learning episodes requires students to recognize and name their nervous system states. This requires neuroception and interoceptive awareness for the sensations from the body to be accurately perceived and processed. Additionally, the co-regulating experience with those involved in the learning episode contributes to feelings of safety or danger. For instance, if a high-stakes test is scheduled for the end of the learning episode, that event may be perceived by the nervous system as a cue of danger.

The Three Cs of Safety, discussed in Chapter 2, also play a role in the emotional states of learners during learning episodes. Students need to feel in control through choices, understand the context for the application or reason for learning the material presented, and experience moments of connection with others within the learning environment.

With awareness of nervous system states and how associated cognitive stories can arise during the learning episode, you can present learning strategies that support learners as they shift into or maintain a ventral vagal state—the optimal state for learning. Techniques for helping students discover ventral resources are discussed in Chapter 4.

REFLECTING ON WHAT YOU'VE LEARNED

- An individual's nervous system influences those of others. We can borrow someone else's regulated nervous system to help bring our own regulation back online. We can also loan our regulated nervous systems to others. Can you think of an example when you've been a borrower or loaner?
- Co-regulation is a biological imperative and comes before self-regulation. Early experiences with co-regulation influence our abilities to co-regulate with others and ultimately self-regulate. Explore a time when you've co-regulated with an infant or child. How did your nervous system respond when the infant or child started to become dysregulated? Did you feel dysregulated, or were you able to stay regulated?
- Interactive regulation is a more inclusive term used to describe regulation that happens from interconnected resources. Does viewing regulation through a more interactive lens support your current understanding of regulation?
- Academic learning theories use the terms self-regulated learning, co-regulated learning, and socially shared regulated learning to explain cognitive processes learners use to reach academic goals. What learning theories underpin how you teach or how you structure lessons?
- Explicitly teaching students about their nervous system states during academic emotional learning phases is an effective way to integrate Polyvagal Theory into learning models.

APPLYING WHAT YOU'VE LEARNED

ACTIVITY ONE: The Ventral Replay

An important aspect of applying Polyvagal Theory is to revisit uncomfortable (but not traumatic) situations and view them through a ventral lens. This serves as a way to see a situation from a different nervous system point of view. Explore a situation where you observed or were part of an event where sympathetic or dorsal states dominated the experience. Now, revisit the event bringing ventral energy into the experience. How could the situation have played out differently when viewed from a ventral vagal state?

ACTIVITY TWO: Understanding Interactive Regulation

Self-regulation is an experience of tapping into regulatory energy from inside ourselves, outside in the environment, and between others in relationships. In this moment, list your available resources. Create three columns with the headings inside myself, outside in my environment, and between myself and others in relationships. Complete the chart and notice where the gaps are. How can you fill those gaps to create more resources?

ACTIVITY THREE: Observing Emotions During
Academic Emotional Learning Phases

The academic emotional learning phases bring the role of emotions into learning theories and expand the models to emotions students experience before, during, and after a learning episode. Observe one of your students during a learning episode, list the emotions you've witnessed, and align the emotions with nervous system states.

CHAPTER 4

Resilience, Relationships, and Reality

et's revisit Green Acres one last time as a perfect prologue to this chapter on the holy grail of surviving and thriving in this world: resilience. Fortunately, I wasn't fired after Principal Parker presented the facts surrounding the paper airplane incident. He and I discussed the unfortunate experience, and created a plan to move forward. With a couple of subsequent visits to my classroom, Dr. Smith regained confidence in my teaching abilities after observing students in a safe and engaging learning environment. We mended the slats in our broken fence—completing an important relationship repair essential for building resilience.

The Reparative Continuum

Polyvagal Theory offers a way forward when experiencing what's referred to in the lexicon of psychology as the *rupture*—or *mismatch* (Dana, 2018; Tronick & Gold, 2020). Ruptures or mismatches happen routinely between people in relationships. Understanding and employing a reparative process is the key to resilience and maintaining healthy relationships.

In the insightful book, *The Power of Discord*, Drs. Tronick and Gold

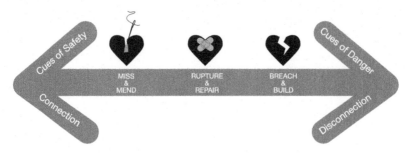

FIGURE 4.1   THE REPARATIVE CONTINUUM
(in collaboration with Leanna Rae, 2022)

use the terms *quotidian* or *everyday resilience* to describe the type of resilience we all need to get through each day. "Resilience develops when you muddle through the inevitable countless mismatches that occur in relationships with people you love, beginning in early infancy" (Tronick & Gold, 2020, p. 132).

When safety, connection, and ventral energy are running in the foreground, there's more tolerance for day-to-day mismatches. In order to understand how mismatches grow into disconnection and how the threat of danger deepens, let's examine the reparative continuum (Figure 4.1).

The reparative continuum demonstrates three types of mismatches: misses, ruptures, and breaches. The ends of the continuum represent the level of threat perceived by the nervous system, ranging from no perceived threat on one end (safety and connection) to a profound threat on the other end (danger and disconnection).

Miss and Mend

Miss and mend refers to missed opportunities to connect that happen in the moments of the day. Confrontations and uncomfortable situations arise, whether we've experienced someone else's biological rudeness, made an insensitive comment to a loved one, or barked at a family member for leaving dishes in the sink. Sometimes we've unintentionally experienced moments of disconnection when expectations aren't met or nervous system needs don't align.

When opportunities are missed, taking a few moments to meet and mend helps remedy feelings of disconnection and lowers the sense of danger. Moments of misses don't need to build into bigger events requiring more reparative energy. Noticing another's closed body language, their Social Engagement System going offline, or seeing them bristle may indicate that there's a miss in the midst. These situations are resolved by acknowledging the miss. Then mending can be as easy as a smile, a compliment, acknowledging someone's feelings, or a "way to go" sticker on a worksheet.

When misses aren't mended, they can turn into microaggressions. Just like annoying paper cuts, microaggressions are a painful reminder that keeps the nervous system on edge. And just like a bandage makes a paper cut feel better, the antidote for microaggressions is the reparative experience of mending the misses.

Rupture and Repair

Ruptures carry more weight on the danger side of the safety scale (see Figure 2.3). When experiencing ruptures, there's a deeper sense of disconnection. Examples of ruptures at school include outbursts of behavior that could injure someone, such as throwing a chair or students aggressively pushing one another. A student verbally insulting a teacher or a dysregulated adult in the room making students feel unsafe moves the mismatch down the continuum into the category of ruptures where the signals of danger intensify, and people begin to disconnect in order to feel safe.

The communication gap widens, and the behavior may worsen the longer the rupture is left untended. Depending upon the severity of the rupture, school administrators, counselors, specialists, or community mental health professionals may need to be involved to move the reparative process along.

Breach and Build

Breaches are intense situations outside societal norms of expected behavior where trust is broken, or people are severely harmed, physically and/or emotionally. Breaches require law enforcement, mental health experts, or specialized trauma teams to respond and intervene to keep people safe and assist in rebuilding from the ground up. The reparative process may include individuals, families, schools, communities, and/or agencies (local, state, and federal). The tragic and alarming increase in school violence is an example of a breach that takes an enormous amount of reparative energy for students and staff to feel safe again and reconnect with one another, school, and community.

Breaches stem from deeper psychological and mental health issues. Experts in mental health focus on understanding the attachment patterns of those they are supporting in therapy and then applying therapeutic methodologies. The term *attachment* refers to infants forming close bonds with their primary caregivers (Chen, 2019). These early bonds create the foundation for healthy social and emotional behavior patterns. Drs. Kain and Terrell, authors of *Nurturing Resilience*, state, "Without access to healthy attachment, consistent co-regulation, and the related sense of safety these produce, the neurophysiological platforms for self-regulation may be disrupted, resulting in dysregulation, or impairment of regulatory mechanisms" (2018, p. 75).

Our life experiences come together to form a metaphorical map of what the nervous system deems safe or dangerous. Heightened events perceived as dangerous are integrated into complex personal patterns therapists call *danger maps*. People who have experienced developmental trauma (ongoing childhood abuse, neglect, or violence) have highly developed danger maps (Kain & Terrell, 2018).

Without experiences of safety and co-regulation, even experiences we've designed to feel inclusive and safe in the classroom may register as dangerous on a student's danger map. The key is to pay attention to students' Social Engagement Systems for signs of discomfort, go slowly, and move incrementally. Redrawing students' danger maps is a process that involves stretching the nervous system just enough and then returning to a comfortable place of safety and connection.

It's impossible to place every type of incident or event neatly onto the continuum in the categories of misses, ruptures, or breaches because responses to situations vary depending on the context and our individual histories. Thus, the continuum is a personalized experience depending on the state of the nervous system and the impact of cognitive stories.

Situations that create disconnection with another person have their roots in our CLA layering processes and the stories our minds create based on our myths, themes, assumptions, values, and beliefs. The perceived severity of a situation depends on how our nervous systems respond and the memories we've tapped into at the time. We can bring conscious awareness to moments of disconnection, but there are times when the nervous system responds automatically to keep us protected. In those situations, the reins are turned over to the ANS until the threat is resolved and safety returns.

Implications for the Classroom

There's a tendency in schools to measure progress at specific set times, like every eight weeks, during report card completion, or at the end of the year. An important, impactful shift for all of us in education is to embrace the notion that the magic happens in moments—not in weeks, months, quarters, or at the end of a school year. Sometimes it's a moment of connection, a moment of meeting and mending, a moment of just being present that teaches the nervous system how to feel safe and regulated. As we discussed earlier, when offering opportunities for connection, a reparative olive branch may or may not be received. Know that it's enough to offer. We all reach out for the branch at different times depending on the available ventral vagal resources required for the mending process. For example, imagine a scenario in which a student tries to talk with you about a situation and you're too busy with other students to acknowledge the student's concern. You notice later in the day that the student isn't participating in class and appears angry. Taking a moment to mend the miss by simply acknowledging that miss can slide both the student and you back to the side of safety and connection on the reparative continuum. The student may remain angry for a day or two. And that's okay. You've initiated the reparative process. It's up to the student to engage.

Understand that what may feel like a miss to you may be a rupture to the other person, and vice versa. The sympathetic storm incident at Green Acres was an example of a rupture, much bigger than a missed opportunity for connection, but not as severe as a breach for my nervous system. Yours may have seen it differently.

Safety Rest Stops

Just as going on a long journey requires the use of a rest stop from time to time, the same is true with a student's journey from danger to safety. A safety rest stop is a place for pausing, taking a break, and bringing ventral energy on board. Safety rest stops include easily accessible and predictable places, people, or things that support regulation. Offering safe opportunities to co-regulate with one another is a good starting point for redrawing danger maps. It's the redrawing process that retunes the nervous system and creates the path to resilience.

Viewing our nervous systems (and those of our students) through a ventral lens retunes them and changes our cognitive stories. A new story appears as the nervous system is reshaped. Like the spelling gene, resilience is often thought of as something you have, or you don't have. This simply isn't true. There's a lot of focus in schools on students' ACE scores (Adverse Childhood Experiences, a measurement of the types of trauma experienced in childhood) (Jennings, 2019b). The impact of an ACE score depends on one's nervous system, the associated cognitive stories, and the extent resilience is developed through the retuning process.

This is the essence of the fourth principle.

PRINCIPLE FOUR: Resilience develops through retuning the nervous system.

Retuning is about doing small, positive things over and over—rather than making big shifts in behavior. I'm often reminded of this when Shalea and I meet monthly with her cognitive-behavioral therapist. He's my step counter, measuring Shalea's progress toward resilience in small, incremental steps rather than big leaps. Don't underestimate the cumulative power of small steps! The best part is that we don't have to develop resilience alone. Resilience develops by building the capacity to return to a ventral state while in relationships with others. We can tap into resilient resources if we know where to find them.

Shared Resilience

One day while walking back to class after lunch, I observed a student sitting on the playground, angry and refusing to get up. The paraprofessional on duty was trying to coax her to stand and return to class. As if embedded in concrete, the student refused to budge. With a few minutes to spare before my next reading group, I asked for permission to intervene. With visible relief, the para turned to me, with an audible "Good luck!" before leaving the playground.

Mirroring the child's body language, I sat beside her on the playground while acknowledging her feelings of anger that recess had ended, and she needed to go back to class. We sat together as I loaned her my regulated nervous system and calm presence. When I sensed an opportunity for connection, I began doing a rhythmic calming routine I teach all my students (one they remind me to use for myself from time to time). Watching me, she began doing the routine. In less than a minute, I heard her sigh and saw her shoulders relax. I asked if she was ready to join her friends. We stood up together, laughing, and skipped our way back to class. Instead of focusing on her cognitive story, I'd focused on the state of her nervous system. When the state changed from sympathetic fight, and ventral energy along with her Social Engagement System came back online, the story changed from "I'm not leaving this playground, no way, no how" to "Let's join my friends in class." Teaching the student something predictable, like the calming routine, supports the nervous system's retuning process.

We co-regulated our way back to a ventral vagal state and into the classroom while adding some capital to the student's resiliency bank. Each time she's able to transition from outside playful energy to a more focused energy needed for the classroom, her nervous system is increasing its flexibility and retuning itself—this is the cornerstone of resilience.

Polyvagal Theory views resilience as something supported by our physiology (Porges, 2017). One important aspect of being resilient is a flexible nervous system that finds its way back from dysregulation to regulation. Just like loaning or borrowing someone's nervous system to help regulate, you can also tap into another person's resilience. Shared resilience helps with moving forward when feeling stuck or when a situation is too overwhelming to handle alone. Reaching out to another and borrowing their resiliency resources and ventral energy builds your resilience as well. It's the back-and-forth sharing that strengthens those resources in ourselves and others.

Triggers and Glimmers

Using the concept of triggers and glimmers helps us monitor our nervous systems and discover ventral resources throughout the day (Dana, 2018). Triggers are those little (and not so little) annoyances and disruptions that make it difficult to remain regulated. By day's end, we can usually recount the triggers with relative ease (trash not taken out, a rude comment from a stranger, or a student's persistent disruptive attitude).

Glimmers, on the other hand, are those moments of pleasure or joy that can serve as a safety rest stop on our danger maps (Dana, 2018). Glimmers are micromoments or small rays of ventral energy—as simple as pausing for a moment to look at greenery just outside the window, noticing the pretty color in a scarf someone is wearing, or observing the smile on a student's face.

We're wired to detect danger and negativity in an effort to keep us out of harm's way. The process of noticing beauty in the ordinary is a positive, nervous system–stretching activity. It takes practice to notice the sprinkling of ventral energy around us. If you do get triggered despite your best efforts, savoring micromoments is a predictable way to reset your nervous system. Providing predictability in the classroom is an important support for your students' nervous systems. Knowing there is a predictable process through the reparative continuum increases safety and offers guidance for how to reconnect when disconnection happens.

When triggered, co-regulating with another person may become a glimmer and nourish the nervous system. At other times, being alone is more beneficial. Knowing there are options between co-regulation or going it alone increases the likelihood of finding the path back to the ventral state—participating in the active process of stretching and retuning the nervous system.

Helping students understand and discover predictability in an unpredictable world settles the nervous system and increases resilience. For instance, students find predictability in the fact that the morning bell rings each day at the same time. Students begin the school day with an opening ritual. Materials are consistently located in designated places. The day ends with a closing group activity.

It's the predictable, repeatable moments that build resilience. Being aware of glimmers and being able to spot them in the environment and in connection with other people increases the internal protective factors (an individual's own personal characteristics) and external protective factors (interactions between individuals, their environment, and relationships) that are essential qualities for being resilient.

Protective Factors Supporting Academic Resilience

The resilience paradigm, increasingly popular in the last two decades, moves the attention from disorders and dysfunctions to understanding what occurs in the lives of people who persevere or thrive socially, emotionally, and academically, despite experiencing adverse life situations (Nicoll, 2014).

How does Polyvagal Theory intersect with the science of academic resilience? Although no universal definition of academic resilience spans all disciplines, it is generally accepted that in the face of long-term adversity or disadvantaged backgrounds, students can adapt and perform well academically despite being exposed to high-risk situations (Beri & Kumar, 2018; Yavuz & Kutlu, 2016; Ye et al., 2021).

Examples of high-risk situations include poverty, abuse (verbal, mental, physical, neglect), experiencing violence, insecure home base (high mobility, parental absence), or natural disasters (Yavuz & Kutlu, 2016). Research studies provide a strong link between academic resilience and higher test scores and grades (McTigue et al., 2009; Rao & Krishnamurthy, 2018).

Research focusing on academic resilience shows clear distinction between resilient and less resilient students. Resilient students have access to a combination of internal and external protective factors (Beri & Kumar, 2018; García-Crespo et al., 2021; Yavuz & Kutlu, 2016).

Examples of internal protective factors include:

- internal locus of control and strong interpersonal skills
- motivation and confidence in ability to complete tasks
- self-efficacy and problem-solving skills
- sense of optimism, hopefulness, and humor
- cognitive flexibility
- planning, organization, and executive functioning skills

- self-confidence in reading
- feelings of belonging to the school

Examples of external protective factors include:

- support from families before starting elementary school
- high expectations from schools that include support to meet those expectations
- participation in school, youth, and religious activities outside the classroom
- positive school environments including programs designed to increase safety on campus
- teaching conflict resolution and social skills
- supportive and caring environments fostering a sense of community
- positive relationships with teachers
- friendships between students and healthy peer relationships

Interestingly, in one study peer connectedness and student hopefulness correlated to academic resilience more significantly than did instructor–student relationships (Frisby et al., 2020). However, in another focusing on high-achieving students in foster care, adults played a significant role in the students' success. Because adults provided emotional support, guidance, and stability, students experienced academic success, including the ability to graduate from high school and be accepted in top-tier universities (Neal, 2017). The bottom line: Positive, supportive friendships and relationships are foundational for academic resilience.

Academic Buoyancy

The research describes academic resilience as relevant to chronic underachievement associated with the lack of internal and external protective factors (Martin & Burns, 2014). *Academic buoyancy* refers to the day-to-day experiences of minor setbacks like a low grade, feeling unmotivated in a particular situation, the stress of an upcoming test, or dealing with a critical review of a paper (Martin & Marsh, 2009). Buoyancy in short bursts leads to the resilience needed for the long haul.

In alignment with Polyvagal Theory, the evidence suggests that it's the human connections within familial, peer-to-peer, and student-teacher relationships that positively impact internal and external protective factors leading to increased academic resilience (Liew et al., 2018; Romano et al., 2021). Ending inequity in the classroom begins with the understanding that academic resilience can be developed and strengthened when prioritized as an important part of the curriculum (Bueno, 2021).

Words and phrases like *bounce back, grit, beating the odds*, and *rising to the occasion* often describe a student with academic resilience and buoyancy. As we've discussed throughout this chapter, the reparative and retuning process brings a deeper meaning to these words and phrases. It's the moment-by-moment connections, repairs of disconnection, and an increased sense of safety that build buoyancy and create the ability for students to bounce back, beat the odds, and experience resilience. This is where the fields of academic resilience and Polyvagal Theory find common ground. Resilience isn't a character trait that students either have or don't have but rather an ongoing, developing process in which befriending and retuning the nervous system plays a starring role.

Cultivating Skills of Academic Resilience

You've designed an incredible lesson and can't wait to share it with your students. Come time to deliver your well-developed activity, all the students are motivated and engaged. You stand a little taller and give yourself an imaginary pat on the back. But then, out of the corner of your eye, you see a student slouched over the desk and disengaged.

You go through a polyvagal checklist in your head to figure out why the student is disengaged:

✓ The classroom environment feels safe enough to engage.
✓ The Three Cs of Safety (choice, context, connection; as described by Deb Dana) are in place. I made sure to include these elements in my lesson plan.
✓ My Social Engagement System is online, sending signals of safety to my students.
✓ Students appear to be in good spirits and enjoying ventral learning at the tops of their ladders.

So what's going on? As you approach the student and begin asking questions, it's clear the student just doesn't want to do the assignment. Both of you are calm, regulated, and socially engaged as you discuss the situation. The student shares that the assignment is a bit overwhelming and would like the opportunity to complete it with the help of a fellow classmate. Impressed with the student's ability to ask for what the nervous system needs at the time, you verbally reinforce their progress toward being more academically resilient, "It's great that you asked for what you needed while staying calm. You recognized feelings of unease and came up with a solution. I appreciate you talking so openly with me."

After you create a safe environment and connect through meaningful relationships, the cultivation begins. The *Oxford English Dictionary* (Oxford University Press, n.d.) defines *cultivate* as the process of acquiring or developing a friendship, attitude, quality, sentiment, or skill. *Cultivate* also means to prepare and use land for growing crops. Both definitions work for this analogy. Think of a regulated nervous system as the prepared soil, and the skills as the plants that grow in the tended soil through nourishing relationships. It's the cultivation of skills that helps retune the nervous system, leading to increased resilience.

Sometimes, students (and our children) just refuse to do what we ask of them. And it may not be due to feeling unsafe, disconnected, or dysregulated. Drs. Tronick and Gold explain the messiness of human relationships and the reality that we're seldom perfectly in sync with others: "Embracing the inevitable muddled, untidy nature of moment-to-moment interactions, creating space to be alone together with others, offers a path of meaningful engagement in the world" (2020, p. 107). Understanding that discord is part of healthy relationships explains the messiness of complicated classrooms where 20 or more nervous systems are expected to hum along in polyvagal bliss. There will be conflicts, as you well know. Still, within regulation, there's room to cultivate the skills necessary to resolve conflict and develop inner protective resources (Rae, personal communication, 2022).

Part of resolving conflicts is the ability, through discord, to participate in healthy discussions and controversy while remaining in a ventral vagal state—a skill essential to bridge the ever-increasing divide between individuals and groups who see the world through different lenses.

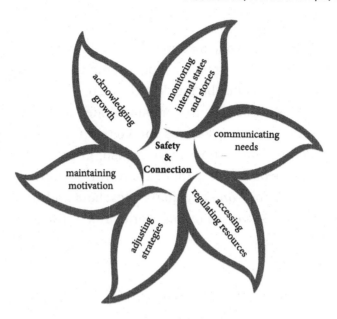

FIGURE 4.2   THE CULTIVATION OF SKILLS

Cultivation is generally a ventral word that brings positive images of growth to mind. In the fertile soil of safety and connection, we cultivate skills that support academic resiliency (Figure 4.2). For instance, examples of skills related to the application of Polyvagal Theory in the classroom include:

- monitoring nervous system states along with cognitive stories
- communicating needs
- accessing regulating resources
- adjusting strategies
- maintaining motivation
- acknowledging growth

The cultivation of skills is contextual and changes depending on the goals for your students. For instance, when using a social–emotional learning curriculum, cultivate the skills outlined in the guidelines. Trauma-sensitive or trauma-informed skills may align with mindfulness, compassion, and cooperation. Discover the skills that work best for your unique situation and objectives.

Some days, it feels like we're cultivating a field of messy mud. The secret is to be able to keep one foot on the ventral rung of the ladder while students are pulling on your other foot, hoping to drag you down your Autonomic Ladder and into the muck with them.

In Chapter 5, we'll be learning about blended states and additional ways to tap into ventral resources for yourself and your students—ultimately spending more time on your lush, grassy ventral path and less time trudging around in the mud. There's also another angle regarding academic resilience—one key quality teachers and students need to be resilient in today's ever-changing world. You'll discover what this is in Chapter 5.

REFLECTING ON WHAT YOU'VE LEARNED

- The reparative continuum includes misses, ruptures, and breaches. As you move across the continuum, your sense of danger increases, and you become more disconnected in a relationship. Does working along a continuum provide more clarity as to when you can resolve a situation on your own or when you need to ask for help from other professionals on your staff or in your community?

- Though we tend to measure our students' accomplishments and growth at particular points in time, it's the micromoments of repeated safety, predictability, and connection that change the nervous system over time. Have you noticed micromoments of growth and positive change in yourself or your students? If so, when? Share an example.

- Academic resilience, though often thought of as something people either have or don't have, can be strengthened through nervous system retuning. Thinking of resilience in terms of expanding nervous system flexibility is a polyvagal approach. Does this align with what you know about building resilience?

- Noticing triggers is a way to bring awareness of those little moments that cause dysregulation for the nervous system. Glimmers are moments of ventral energy that help us find regulation. Do you have your own terms for triggers and glimmers? If so, what are those terms, and do you prefer one term over another?

APPLYING WHAT YOU'VE LEARNED

ACTIVITY ONE: Experiencing the Reparative Continuum

Draw a reparative continuum on a piece of paper and carry it with you for one day. Consciously notice when there are signs of danger or disconnection in your relationships. Jot down examples of misses, ruptures, and breaches (hopefully no breaches!). Note how you handled each of the reparative opportunities and how that felt for your nervous system.

ACTIVITY TWO: Drawing Your Danger Map and Safety Rest Stops

Those who have experienced trauma can have very complex danger maps. Seemingly innocuous events can be a cue of danger. Draw your own danger map and indicate possible safety rest stops. This can bring awareness to feelings of danger while discovering opportunities to increase your sense of safety.

ACTIVITY THREE: Creating Your Triggers and Glimmers Summary

At the end of a day, create a triggers and glimmers summary. Draw a line down the middle of a sheet of paper. On one side, list the triggers that crept into your day. On the other side, list the glimmers that helped bring ventral energy back into your system. Then divide your glimmers list into two columns. The first column should include the glimmers shared with others and the other, glimmers you felt alone.

ACTIVITY FOUR: Designing a Glimmer Gallery

Explain the concept of glimmers to students and teach them how to look for glimmers throughout their school day. At the end of the day, create a glimmers gallery. Have each student say, draw, or write down one glimmer they experienced. Share the glimmers with the class (optional, not required) and add them to a glimmer gallery. This can be simply a space on a whiteboard, a place on a bulletin board, or an individual booklet each student adds to daily. Noticing glimmers at the end of the day is a positive way to connect with each other and learn more about glimmer resources you can make available for your students and yourself. Noticing glimmers helps build resilience!

CHAPTER 5

Anchored and Adaptable Learners

Remember the sinking boat story that I shared in the introduction? What you've learned to this point provides the resources needed to stop taking in water and drowning your enthusiasm and passion for teaching. Just as a boat needs an anchor to remain safely in port, your nervous system needs anchoring to be safely tethered to regulating ventral resources.

Anchors Leading to Adaptability

Repeatable and predictable micromoments of beauty, connection, support, and safety become anchors so you can engage with the world from a place of optimism, hope, and curiosity. The process called anchoring helps move us from protection and back to connection. Ventral anchors include the people, things, places, and times in your life that bring you joy (Dana, 2018).

These anchors are established or experienced when you're in the ventral vagal state at the top of the Autonomic Ladder and help you remain steady when you're later caught in an unexpected storm or choppy waters. Having some slack in the rope from the anchor to the boat provides for movement in and out of your nervous system states while being able to stay anchored in ventral or at least keep ventral in view.

What makes it possible to accept change, view situations from different angles, or transition from one course of action to another? In a word, adaptability. In the school setting, adaptability is defined as "appropriate cognitive, behavioral, and/or affective adjustments in the face of uncertainty and novelty" (Martin et al., 2013). It's how students learn to act in a manner suited to a new environment.

Research suggests adaptability and resilience share a kindred relationship (Martin & Burns, 2014). In the application of Polyvagal Theory, resilience and adaptability depend on a responsive, flexible nervous system that adapts to unexpected and novel situations. When staff and students are resilient and adaptable, classrooms feel more hopeful. This optimism is reflected in academic outcomes as well (Frisby et al., 2020). The ability to move in and out of nervous system states while knowing how to access ventral resources is an important aspect of being resilient and adaptable.

PRINCIPLE FIVE: Adaptability relies on access to ventral resources.

Discovering Ventral Resources (adapted from Dana, 2018)

Who. Think about the people in your life who are steadfast and there for you when needed. These special people make you feel seen, appreciated, and loved. Pets can certainly be anchors as well. Your list may extend to a higher power, spiritual guides, or people who have passed. These people, guides, or furry friends live in your heart and travel with you wherever you go. As teachers, we may be the "who" or the predictable anchor in the lives of our students until we cultivate the capacity for them to discover their own anchors.

What. What things in your life bring you joyful energy? Look for those moments when you feel relaxed, nourished, or alive in the present moment. Is it a good cup of coffee, an enjoyable book, or a conversation with a friend?

When. Think about times in your life when you've felt joy, contentment, or flow. Bring those memories to life by revisiting the event in your mind and feeling the positive energy in your body.

Where. When you feel regulated, where are you? Perhaps you're on your back porch watching a sunset, taking a walk in your neighborhood, or sitting at your local coffee shop.

Anchors are contextual, meaning they change depending on the situation. Ventral anchors at school may be different than ventral anchors at home. Wherever you go, knowing you are safely tethered by your anchors is an important step toward adapting to the unexpected challenges and novelties of the day.

By being safely moored in ventral vagal, you're able to communicate safety to others and share your regulated nervous system. Expressing compassion—an inner resource—is only possible when in a ventral state. When you're away from your ventral home in a sympathetic or dorsal vagal state, your anchors guide you back home to ventral vagal.

Your Go-To Place Within

When stressed or experiencing nudges of danger, you may move down your ladder. Over time, you've most likely developed a pattern or preference for one state over another, whether it be sympathetic or dorsal vagal. Your tendency to move into one state over another is your default mode—that place you instinctively go to during tough times (what Deb Dana calls your "home away from home").

Begin noticing where you tend to go when you wander off your ventral path. To be clear, one state isn't necessarily better than another. As humans, we're designed to experience the full range of emotions. You might move to your default state to get through a challenging time or respond to an unexpected situation. That's what adaptability is all about—befriending your nervous system and increasing the awareness of your states so you can move with flexibility in and out of states and find your way back to ventral through accessing your anchors.

Sometimes we get caught in a loop where we're trying to get out of one state but end up back in it over and over again. For example, if you're in a dorsal vagal depressed state and manage to find some mobilizing sympathetic energy, it may not be enough to get you back to ventral, so you drop back down into dorsal vagal. Remember, to get out of a dorsal vagal state, we must climb back up the ladder to ventral by going through the mobilizing energy of sympathetic. You can't skip the sympathetic rungs of the ladder. Sympathetic energy is generally a disorganized form of mobilization. A gentle walk is an example of bringing ventral energy into the system that can help move a person out of the dorsal–sympathetic loop.

You may also find yourself in a loop of sympathetic and ventral vagal with too much energy flooding your system and not enough ventral resources to keep you in ventral vagal. Whether you're caught in a loop or have wandered off your ventral path, head back to ventral by accessing your regulating resources. Like most change, this takes time and practice. Remember, big changes are just a series of small steps strung together over time.

Adaptability and the Vagal Brake

By retuning the nervous system and redrawing danger maps (as discussed in Chapter 4), we operationalize the process of being adaptable. The *vagal brake* is the heart's built-in pacemaker (the sinoatrial node), Without the vagal brake, the heart would beat at about 90 beats per minute, too fast to maintain over a long period of time. With the influence of the vagal brake, the heart rate slows to about 72 beats per minute in order to keep a safer rhythm (Dana, 2018). The vagal brake, through engagement and disengagement via the vagal pathway to the heart, slows or speeds the heart as needed for increasing adaptability and makes transitioning from more active activities to calmer activities possible. The ability to calm down after recess or after doing an active classroom activity depends on a well-functioning vagal brake.

When working well, the vagal brake releases to allow more energy and reengages to provide calming energy to maintain ventral vagal regulation (Porges, 2021). The vagal brake is responsible for increasing nervous system flexibility and adaptability. However, due to their complex danger maps, people with histories of trauma often experience a vagal brake that doesn't allow nuanced mobilizing or calming energy to enter the system.

Blended States and Learning

The vagal brake is active during the *blended state of play*. It allows us to move, laugh, and co-regulate during play. Your ability to rev up and rev down relies on the functioning of your vagal brake. Think of the childhood game of Red Light, Green Light where you run when someone calls out "green" and stop when someone calls out "red." This is a good example of the vagal brake in action, with the heart rate increasing and decreasing as needed to remain in a playful state (Greene, personal communication, 2022).

Classrooms are a series of Red Light, Green Light situations. We constantly ask students to start and then stop. We expect students to monitor their energy levels to stay in their optimal learning zones. It takes a well-adjusted vagal brake to keep up with the constant change from high-energy activities to lower-energy activities. If we mix in some yellow light in between, this offers a smoother transition between red and green. Providing a countdown of some sort warning students of an imminent change is an easy way to add moments of yellow to transitions. Some teachers and their students sing clean-up songs or have transition rituals. This helps

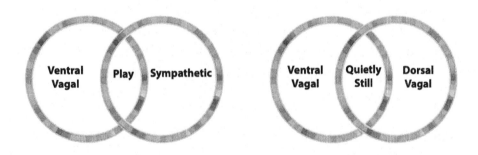

FIGURE 5.1   ANS BLENDED STATES

learners adjust their vagal brakes in order to successfully negotiate the frequent red and green lights in the classroom.

The Blended State of Play

Play is part of every culture and brings people together. Safe and interactive play is also part of our childhood history, teaching our nervous systems how to move from calmness into activity and back again. Play shapes our brains and bodies from childhood through adulthood.

According to Porges (2017), "Polyvagal Theory defines interactive play as a 'neural exercise' that enhances co-regulation of physiological state to promote the neural mechanisms involved in supporting mental and physical health" (p. 22). Play is a combination of the ventral vagal Social Engagement System accompanied by sympathetic mobilizing energy. When ventral and sympathetic are in a symbiotic relationship, play is safe and enjoyable. With your vagal brake working as designed, you can now access mobilized energy without a full-blown sympathetic response, allowing you to move in meaningful ways. Examples of organized mobilization include participating in an aerobics class, taking a restorative walk in the park, or wrestling with your children.

For people who have experienced trauma, play may be perceived by the nervous system as a sign of danger because of the spontaneous nature of interacting with others in a way that requires autonomic flexibility, maintaining connection, co-regulating with others, and keeping the Social Engagement System online. If the sympathetic nervous system decides to go it alone without ventral vagal, the interaction shifts from playfulness to dysregulation or aggression. When feelings of safety increase and signs of danger decrease, play stretches the nervous system and increases flexibility.

Increasing Joy Through Play

By the time Shalea turned four, every day consisted of regimented therapy routines. I felt more like a rehabilitation therapist than a mother. Shalea resisted the exercises, and I dreaded doing them with her.

We attended a workshop with an occupational therapist known for her novel approach to therapy. During class, her joyful way of relating to the children led them down the merry path of participation and cooperation—laughter filling the room. I wanted to bottle and take home some of her magical fairy dust.

While conversing during lunch, I told the therapist about our daily, grueling therapy routines and how we struggled to complete them as prescribed. Looking at me with kind eyes and a dimpled smile, she said three words: "Make it play."

At home and school, a new joyful path of learning emerged. With new-found enthusiasm and motivation, I infused therapy sessions at home and literacy lessons at school with playful, engaging activities.

One day, while my students were actively participating in literacy stations that looked more like play than serious reading intervention, a student walking down the hall on her way to places unknown, peeked inside my classroom, and asked, "Ms. Wilson, how do I get to come to your class?" I thought, "Well, just have a dreadful time with reading and writing, and you'll end up here." Filtering, I replied, "That's the nicest compliment anyone's ever paid me! It makes me happy that you want to come to my class. Maybe you can stop by tomorrow during recess, and I'll invite one of my students to teach you some of the activities."

Having students investigate our classrooms and want to come inside is a worthwhile objective for any teacher. I needed to get creative to address my students' variety of focusing, executive functioning, developmental, behavioral, emotional, and academic issues. Engaging, purposeful move-ment activities accompanied literacy centers. As students rotated through centers, they actively bounced balls while reciting words, sat on gym balls during partner reading, or recited vocabulary words while rhyth-mically tapping on each one using alternating right and left hands. What looked like play to the student peeking into my room was serious learning grounded in neuroscience supporting co-regulating, rhythmic activities, and sensory-based movement.

One of the most powerful insights I've gained from understanding Polyvagal Theory is recognizing that students in a sympathetic state have disorganized, mobilized energy. However, when we integrate elements of safe, organized play and hands-on learning into the curriculum, students move into regulation with relative ease.

Learning while in a state of play requires clear guidelines, a proper balance of discipline and freedom; encouragement and boundaries. It's within rules and guidelines that we nurture the positive interactions of play. At times, play needs to be strategically designed to produce a particular outcome (in class); at other times, it can be unstructured (recess or home).

Play often leads to laughter, and laughter produces a long list of benefits, including lowering stress, reducing signs of depression, reducing pain levels, increasing endorphins, dissipating hostility, strengthening bonds in relationships, improving retention of learned concepts, and enhancing conflict resolution (Cozolino, 2013; Nasr, 2013).

Friendships often develop through play and laughter; and as noted previously, friendships are a protective resource on the path to resilience. The evolution of play from infancy through adulthood is a blended state of mind and body requiring the ability to adapt to novel experiences and changes within the maturing continuum of friendships. "In adolescence, play turns into hanging around. Sharing turns into helping. Loyalty and intimacy become more central requirements, especially for best friends. Friends become important sources of validation and support" (Denworth, 2020, p. 93).

With the focus in today's schools on students being calm and quiet, we're missing out on the important benefits of the blended state of play. While there may be times when students need to be calm and quiet, be sure to integrate a good dose of purposeful play into your curricula to increase active, co-regulating, autonomic toning opportunities for all learners. Calm and active are not mutually exclusive. Students can participate in mobilizing activities while remaining calm. That's the power of the vagal brake and blending calming energy of ventral vagal with the mobilizing energy of sympathetic.

In my experience, it's much easier to wrangle disorganized, mobilized energy through structured movement and play than it is to immobilize the energy altogether through quieting activities. And there's a good reason for this observation, as explained by the second blended state that intertwines the top and bottom rungs of the ladder, making it a big leap metaphorically and physiologically for the nervous system.

The Blended State of Quietly Still

The blended state of *quietly still* doesn't require engagement and disengagement of the vagal brake because there's no sympathetic mobilization during the quietly still state. The ventral vagal state blended with dorsal vagal allows for stillness without going into a full dorsal shutdown.

Sitting with someone and being comfortable in silence, enjoying intimacy with another person, or lying next to someone while sleeping are examples of how the intertwining of ventral vagal and dorsal vagal states creates the blended state of quietly still.

Mindfulness and meditation are also examples of being in a quietly still state. Mindfulness is defined as "paying attention to the present moment with acceptance and nonjudgment" (Willard, 2016, p. 33). Another similar definition is "awareness of the present moment with an attitude of curiosity and openness" (Jennings, 2019a, p. 121). Though there are many different forms of mindfulness and meditative practices, the most difficult to achieve are those requiring quiet and stillness. An enormous amount of safety from within and from the environment is required to move into a quietly still state.

For people who have experienced trauma, trying to feel safe while in a still state may elicit a protective response. A co-regulating partner or mental health professional can increase feelings of safety and help integrate the new insights gained when expanding the window of awareness through mindfulness or meditative practices (Rae, personal communication, 2022).

If a person is in the sympathetic state with disorganized mobilized energy, mindfulness or meditative practices, including breathing exercises, may be difficult to accomplish. Participating in an activity involving organized movement helps the nervous system find regulation and shift into a quieter state.

Dr. Christopher Willard, a psychologist, member of the Harvard Medical School faculty, and author of numerous books on mindfulness, illustrates this point:

> When I was a teacher, I would get home from work, go jogging for half an hour, and immediately sit down to meditate after that. The habit of physical exercise was a simple foundation for

> *mental exercise and also gave me a cognitive boost that helped*
> *me sit in focused quiet.* (2016, p. 49)

With the increased popularity of mindfulness in schools, understanding the requirements of the nervous system at particular moments in time is an important consideration. In the befriending process, knowing what nourishes the nervous system is a principal aspect of applying Polyvagal Theory. For the nervous system to work optimally, it needs a balance of self-regulation and co-regulation, along with playfulness and quiet.

The Freeze Response

There are two different freeze responses generally described by polyvagal practitioners. The first is a blend of sympathetic and dorsal vagal states. The other is a full dorsal vagal response. An example of the blended freeze response is when you experience an unsafe situation requiring an ANS response. For instance, when you see a car barreling toward you, your nervous system may activate a momentary freeze response until a decision is made to jump out of the way (sympathetic). If the situation is perceived as too dangerous, the freeze response may shift into a pure dorsal vagal shutdown response.

Within the context of school, another version of the freeze response is important to understand. When we're rushed and want our students to do something quickly, we may give students many different prompts, one after another. When too much information comes in too rapidly, the nervous system may try to control the number of incoming stimuli by eliciting a freeze response, a combination of sympathetic mobilization with dorsal vagal immobilization.

The freeze response is beyond a student's control. The fast pace of most classrooms makes it difficult for some learners to process the rapid fire of incoming auditory, visual, and sensory information. The nervous system attempts to automatically stop the barrage of incoming sensory stimuli by freezing. From the outside, this looks like a student being stubborn, uncooperative, or noncompliant. There may be frustration on the adult's part at the lack of response to directions or the perceived unwillingness to "get moving!"

Students realize that if they don't do what the teacher asks, they're liable to get into trouble, yet the nervous system is unable to create an organized response. You'll know when the freeze response is activated by observing students' stiffening muscles, eyes wide with fear, and an inability to move. For some, vocalization is possible, and for others language goes offline.

My daughter's default mode is the freeze response. Now that I understand freeze as a nervous system protective response, I simply ask, "Shalea, are you frozen?" She'll manage to give me a thumbs up, her gesture for *yes*. That's my cue to give her a hug. She usually starts crying while we're hugging, and then she's able to release, reconnect, and take steps toward reorganizing her system. Through this co-regulation, she's able to bring ventral back into her system. Shalea and I have designed a ventral anchor reference chart, and my hugs are a ventral resource for her nervous system. This chart is like having a personalized, easily accessible ventral vagal owner's manual that I refer to when her nervous system needs some ventral retuning.

Being aware of the freeze response and observing it in students requires expanding your view of the causality of certain behaviors—often perfectly appropriate and adaptive when one is experiencing too many signals of danger. If freezing isn't acknowledged and supported by offering ventral resources, the student may shut down altogether.

Quietly Failing

When students exhibit a dorsal vagal state, often accompanied by collapsed posture and a give-up-why-bother attitude, I refer to this as a *quietly failing response*. Quietly failing students don't disrupt or shine the light on themselves. They don't engage in challenging behaviors or create conflicts with others. They sit quietly—physically seen but emotionally invisible. They may want to be seen but don't feel safe enough to connect due to developmental trauma or other emotional issues tucked away, hidden from view. They, along with their trauma, prefer to remain unseen. Going slowly and establishing trust are important steps toward connecting with students exhibiting a quietly failing response.

Volumes of books have been written about students with readily observable behaviors, often requiring expert intervention from the school Applied Behavior Analysis staff, school counselor, autism specialist, or behavior specialist. These are the ones you remember while reflecting on your day. They may have pushed some buttons and triggered a nervous system response in you that caused a tumble down a few rungs on your own ladder.

Meanwhile, quietly failing students are aware they're not measuring up—but are too afraid to ask questions or advocate for themselves. We tend to focus less on these students because their behavior doesn't require immediate attention. Their louder and more obvious classmates supersede. And yet, progress eludes them—failing or at risk of failing.

Quietly failing doesn't necessarily mean these learners are uninformed or less capable than other students. What I've come to appreciate is the depth of their quiet wisdom. Even though the words to express their feelings aren't readily within mind's reach, they have an inner understanding of how learning could be for them if only they had a say in the matter—some control over their learning environments.

Quietly failing students may be introverts who prefer listening rather than talking when in a group setting, and they feel safer working solo. Introverts have a rich inner life but may feel threatened, become exhausted, and overwhelmed with too much classroom stimulation or cooperative learning activities (Cain, 2013).

Research supports that extroverts are more successful in classrooms (Beri & Kumar, 2018). Perhaps their success is due more to the design of classroom activities than to qualities associated with extroversion. We need to offer a variety of learning opportunities including activities supporting introverts and their extrovert or ambivert (showing both tendencies) peers. Only when introverts are emotionally seen and supported do they show their qualities and strengths.

Bridging the Failure-Success Gap

A body of research focusing on failure dynamics categorizes learners into three subsets: success oriented, failure avoidant, and failure accepting (Martin et al., 2015). The Motivation and Engagement Wheel is a multidimensional model that has evolved over time and depicts the outcomes of continued research focusing on failure dynamics, resilience, buoyancy, and adaptability (Martin & Burns, 2014).

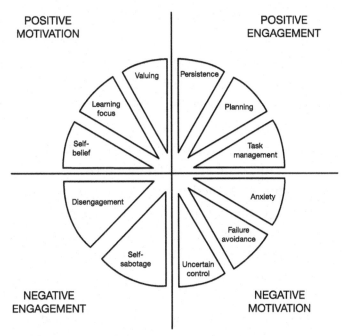

FIGURE 5.2 THE MOTIVATION AND ENGAGEMENT WHEEL
(Reproduced with permission from Dr. Andrew J. Martin and Lifelong
Achievement Group, https://lifelongachievement.com/.)

Dr. Andrew J. Martin, a psychologist and professor at the University
at New South Wales in Australia, is recognized for his psychological and
educational research focusing on motivation, engagement, resilience, and
achievement. With his work being extensively validated and cited across
disciplines, the Motivation and Engagement Wheel provides a solid model
for integrating Polyvagal Theory into educational pedagogy (Figure 5.2).

The top half of the Martin Wheel, positive motivation and positive
engagement, depicts characteristics of success-oriented learners. These
individuals believe in themselves, value school, focus for learning, and
plan accordingly to complete assignments, manage their study habits,
and persist when things get tough. Initially, learning new skills can be
dysregulating, but the success-oriented student knows how to keep ventral in view. Success-oriented learners are in a state of ventral learning
and employ problem-solving strategies when they experience setbacks.

Those students with lower motivation and lower engagement (the bottom half of Martin's Wheel) lack the inner resources to become ventral

learners. These students exhibit signs of being in sympathetic or dorsal vagal states, unaware of how to tap into the resources needed to move to the top half of the Wheel with their positively motivated and engaged peers. Beyond being unaware, possibly the resources to grow their skills aren't available within themselves, in their learning environment, or in relationships with family, friends, and school staff.

As an example, after completing a training, the administrator of a private school took me aside and asked if I'd create a reading lab for their high school students. Intrigued, I visited the vast wooded campus in a small town with nothing but an essentials-only grocery store, church, and a historic motel with an adjacent restaurant. The parents paid a great deal of money to send their teens to this boarding school that promoted outdoor activities and international travel experiences. For most, this was a last-ditch attempt to revive their teens' interest in school.

Before designing the lab, I met with potential reading lab students. With each informal conversation, disillusioned and angry students made clear their beliefs—nothing and no one could help them read and write at grade level. Recurrent themes included, "I'm pretty stupid when it comes to reading and writing." "Everyone's tried to teach me without any luck." And one student, prior to slamming the door on his way out, mumbled, "You're wasting your time." Psychometric tests proved unsurprising—low scores in executive functioning skills, phonemic awareness, auditory memory, visual memory . . . and on it went—a kaleidoscope of challenges contributing to their current self-doubt and lackluster attitudes toward learning.

Let's revisit Martin's Wheel and place these students. They land solidly in the negative engagement and motivation quadrants. In polyvagal terms, their nervous systems exhibit responses common to sympathetic and dorsal vagal states—anger, anxiety, apathy, and hopelessness.

I knew the reading lab had to snag their interest as soon as they walked through its weathered log cabin door, just like the students at Green Acres. The staff and I created novel activities based on their active lifestyles. Everything focused on relevance to their lives and things they found interesting. Teaching included using similar neurodevelopmental and sensory-based strategies that I used with students during my regular teaching job. The students' disorganized, mobilized energy found productive outlets that brought more ventral energy into their systems. Sitting on gym balls while working provided gentle rocking movement that helped some of the failure-accepting students move out of dorsal apathy. As their nervous system states changed, so did their cognitive stories. Their deepest layers of myths about their inability to learn transformed as they participated in ventral learning—optimistic, hopeful, motivated, and engaged.

In retrospect, important polyvagal concepts created the core of the reading lab experience. Supportive, safe relationships between teachers and students facilitated students' movement from the bottom half of Martin's Wheel to the top half. During graduation, many parents commented on the positive changes in their teens—a result of the school's outdoor, active philosophy focusing on teamwork and relationships, complemented by the reading lab experience.

Now let's fill the empty hub of Martin's Wheel with important guiding concepts from the application of Polyvagal Theory and, by doing so, create a working model to begin the implementation process—a worthwhile objective and key focus of this book.

The Polyvagal Learning Hub depicts the importance of students having access to safety, connection, and interactive regulating resources, along with mentors to support cultivating the skills needed for success (Figure 5.3). In addition, I've included the cultivation of skills in this

FIGURE 5.3   THE POLYVAGAL LEARNING HUB

model. As educators, we can support the failure-avoidance or failure-acceptance students by ensuring availability of learning hub resources and then mastering the skills habitual to positively engaged and motivated students. Strategies include increasing the feelings of safety, offering more control through choices, attending to context, and enhancing students' sense of belonging through connection with supportive staff and peers. Co-regulating opportunities with other adults and students willing to share their regulated nervous systems may help cultivate the skills attributed to success-oriented students.

When noticing that a student's nervous system needs safety and regulatory resources, the learning hub is a guide for choosing what resource(s) might provide the best support. It's not possible to provide all the resources in the hub to all students at the same time. Nervous systems need different things at different times. For instance, sometimes a student's nervous system needs a few choices about how to accomplish a learning task independently. At other times, choices can be overwhelming, and what the student needs is simply someone sitting beside them saying, "Let's see what happens when we try this together."

The question students need to learn to ask themselves is, "What do I need right now to keep my head in the game?" If students know how to access and utilize the available resources in the Hub, then they're able to keep their heads and their nervous systems in the learning game—the path to joyful learning begins unfolding before them. This is how we bridge the failure–success gap and create equitable classrooms where all children develop resilience and adaptability.

Moving From Failure Avoidance and Acceptance to Success

Let's summarize how to move students from being failure avoidant and failure acceptant to success oriented in five nervous system–supporting steps:

1. Bring the Polyvagal Learning Hub alive in the classroom. Ensure students have access to the resources in the Hub in order to choose, at any given moment in time, what their nervous system needs to find regulation.
2. Explicitly teach, cultivate, and provide opportunities for the devel-

opment of essential skills including planning, organizing, and management of learning tasks.

3. Begin the befriending process by modeling healthy regulation and encouraging students to learn how to identify their nervous system states during learning episodes, including honing their interoceptive awareness.

4. Introduce the concept of ventral anchors and have students design their own ventral vagal owner's manual.

5. Utilize the CLA framework to deconstruct and reconstruct myths, metaphors, assumptions, and beliefs about learning.

Becoming Adaptable

We become adaptable through our daily opportunities to retune our nervous systems and increase the awareness of our cognitive stories. Real growth toward adaptability occurs through the anchoring and befriending process along with knowing how to access the resources needed to be regulated adults and students in the classroom. That's how we begin transforming classrooms one nervous system at a time, starting with our own!

Our polyvagal journey continues in Chapter 6 as we connect the nervous system with current brain science and expand the popular phrase "mind–body connection" into "mind–body–world connection" (Paul, 2021).

REFLECTING ON WHAT YOU'VE LEARNED

- Ventral vagal anchors help bring you back to the top of your Autonomic Ladder when you are moving down into sympathetic or dorsal vagal nervous system responses (Dana, 2018). Being able to access your anchors is an important process in befriending your nervous system.

- Your default mode is the nervous system state you most frequently visit when things get tough, or when you're stressed or exhausted. Accessing your ventral anchors is a process to find your way back to ventral vagal when you feel yourself moving off your ventral path.

- There are two blended states called *play* and *quietly still*. The vagal brake is active during the blended state of play as the sympathetic and ventral vagal states merge to enable play. Conversely, quietly still is a blended state of ventral vagal and dorsal vagal. This is a difficult state to move into and requires a lot of safety in order to be comfortable while still.

- Some polyvagal theorists recognize a third blended state, freeze. Freeze and quietly failing are both responses that can occur when students are overloaded and need ventral resources. Have you experienced learners who appear to be stubborn or uncooperative? Do you think they might be exhibiting a freeze response? Do you have any students who are quietly failing? Do they concern you as much as the students with overt behaviors?

- The Motivation and Engagement Wheel, created by Dr. Andrew Martin, is a model summarizing extensive research on resilience, buoyancy, and adaptability. The science of failure dynamics places students in three categories: success oriented, failure avoidant, and failure accepting. By integrating the Polyvagal Learning Hub into the Martin Wheel, the model provides additional insights into how to move students from the negative engagement and negative motivation lower level of the Martin Wheel to the positive motivation and engagement upper half of Martin's Wheel. Do you know which students in your classroom are success oriented, failure avoidant, or failure accepting?

APPLYING WHAT YOU'VE LEARNED

ACTIVITY ONE: Creating a Ventral Vagal Anchor Chart

What brings ventral vagal energy alive in you? Complete a list of your who, what, where, and when anchors. You can simply write your responses, but you'll remember them easier if you add some doodles or images to illustrate your anchors. Your anchors can be context specific. If your anchors are chosen within the context of school, share your chart with other staff members or invite them to design their charts at the next staff meeting. Once you're safely anchored in ventral, you'll be able to start the anchoring process with your students.

ACTIVITY TWO: Discovering Your Go-To Place Within

Where do you go when you wander off your ventral path? Next time you find yourself moving into sympathetic or dorsal vagal, reach for your regulating resources to help you find your way back onto your ventral path.

ACTIVITY THREE: Observing Your Students' Go-To Place Within

Throughout the school day, observe your students in action. When challenged or stretched, where is each student's go-to place? What triggers moved them into sympathetic and dorsal vagal states? Which students can find the way back to ventral and which are unable to keep ventral in view? As you observe, are you seeing the value of introducing the concept of ventral anchors to your students? Does knowing their ventral anchors give you more tools to readily support their nervous systems? Move from observation to action by inviting your students to develop personalized ventral regulating resources that they list and access when needed.

CHAPTER 6

The Ventral Path to Joyful Learning

On a jam-packed day, while driving from one appointment to another, I happened to catch a radio interview with Annie Murphy Paul (2021), prolific science journalist and author of *The Extended Mind: The Power of Thinking Outside the Brain*. As she discussed the limitations of the brain, I leaned in and turned up the volume. The science is clear. The brain has limits regarding the amount of information it can take in and process efficiently. With brains on overload, we continue to cram increasing amounts of information into our overworked, tired minds. There's a solution—instead of the brain doing more heavy lifting, share the load.

Let's begin by letting go of all the metaphors describing the brain as the captain of our ships or a muscle that needs a workout. The mind isn't always the captain, nor does it need to work harder. Rather, we should see it as a relational organ relying on the nervous system and resources outside its sophisticated neural circuitry to ultimately become the best version of itself. The mind, by lightening its load, can work more efficiently and flexibly. The nervous system and its role in expanding the brain's capacity is an important focus of this chapter and the sixth polyvagal principle.

> ### PRINCIPLE SIX: Nervous system flexibility underpins cognitive flexibility.

Though the mind–body connection is a common expression, the more accurate description is a mind–body–world connection in which the expression extends to the environment and our relationships with others (Paul, 2021). This is because the brain is a co-regulating, relational, context-generating, story-making organ intimately in relationship with the autonomic nervous system. According to Dana (2021),

> *While we may think our brains are in charge, the heart of our daily experience and the way we navigate the world begins in our bodies with the autonomic nervous system. This is the place where the stories emerge about who we are and how the world works, what we do and how we feel.* (p. 13)

The nervous system creates the foundation for efficient cognitive functioning. That statement may feel like a big shift for those of us with strong allegiance to brain-based teaching and cognitive neuroscience (the development of the mind and brain). Let's remain open to the possibility that we might not have the complete picture when it comes to understanding how to create fertile environments that stimulate growing minds as we explore the relationship between Polyvagal Theory and the popular mindset paradigm. From there, we investigate cognitive load theory, extended mind science (with its three types of cognition), and cognitive flexibility to see how polyvagal concepts align. It's an intriguing CLA experience, sure to challenge some of your myths, assumptions, beliefs, and perceptions about the brain.

A Polyvagal-Guided Approach to Mindsets

Dr. Carol Dweck's (2016) widely read book, *Mindset: The New Psychology of Success*, introduced the terms *fixed mindset* and *growth mindset* to explain why some people outperform others. These terms are commonly used to describe the underlying belief system that people have about their intelligence. People with a growth mindset believe their intelligence can be developed, while people with a fixed mindset believe otherwise. When applied to education, recognizing the difference in these two mindsets was intended to help close achievement gaps by understanding why some students achieve in school while others do not. In a commentary to educators, Dweck, a psychologist at Stanford University, makes this important observation about how educators have implemented the mindset philosophy:

> A growth mindset isn't just about effort. Perhaps the most common misconception is simply equating the growth mindset with effort. Certainly, effort is key for students' achievement, but it's not the only thing. Students need to try new strategies and seek input from others when they're stuck. They need this repertoire of approaches—not just sheer effort—to learn and improve. (Dweck, 2015, p. 20)

Beyond effort, grit, and skills, a growth mindset begins outside the brain, in the ANS pathways. It's here where the mindset seeds are planted through a person's early experiences with safety, choice, connection, co-regulation, and attachment (Kain & Terrell, 2018).

Somewhere between fixed and growth mindsets lies an evolving mindset—a gray space that blends the black-and-white duality of fixed versus growth. Mindsets are contextual; there's a sense of evolution between fixed and growth that's influenced by feeling safe inside our bodies, outside in the environment, and between people in relationships (Figure 6.1).

The learning environment provides a sense of safety or danger. Through neuroception and interoception, learners' built-in stress detectors are fully functioning. Students need to be explicitly taught to monitor the messages coming into the body via the nervous system. Through recognizing and paying attention to those feelings, they're able to notice the niggling inside, alerting them of shifting nervous system states.

Students becoming aware of their nervous system states during academic activities is an important and critical aspect of being success oriented and spending more time on the growth side of the mindset cycle. The states of the nervous system and the accompanying story affect students' beliefs in their abilities to learn.

FIGURE 6.1   THE EVOLVING MINDSET CYCLE

The space between a fixed and growth mindset is the place where students learn how to befriend their nervous systems and monitor their thinking (metacognitive skills) and feelings. All points in between fixed and growth mindsets are accepted and supported. No nervous system state or mindset is inherently wrong—rather, it is responsive, depending on the learning environment and relationships within the learning space.

Take a moment to think about two teachers you had in school. First think about one who made you feel seen and supported. Even if the subject was difficult or not your favorite, you felt safe enough to take risks and stretch past your academic comfort zone. You believed in your ability to learn, and you engaged using a growth mindset. Your teacher held a growth mindset on your behalf as well, believing in your ability to grow your intellect through grasping the course content. With support, connection, and safety, you spent more time in a ventral vagal state than in a sympathetic or dorsal vagal state.

Now think about the teacher who elicited fear, anger, doubt, frustration, or anxiety. Consider your mindset in that classroom. Did you believe in your ability to learn the content? Did your teacher believe in your ability to master the content? Most likely, you experienced feelings associated with sympathetic (fight or flight) or dorsal vagal (shutdown). These two examples illustrate the contextual elements of the mindset paradigm.

Learning is a relational experience, and the relationship between teacher and learner contributes to the mindset cycle.

There are times when students experience setbacks and challenges with content, even with positive relationships and learning environments. And, of course, factors outside of school, beyond a teacher's control, impact learners in the classroom. Teaching students how to recognize and deal with fear of failure, anxiety, and negative emotions during learning episodes are positive strategies to promote an evolving mindset. The needle moves toward the growth side of the mindset cycle.

It's in the aliveness and fluidity of the learning process that we discover, as Dweck (2015) states, "The path to a growth mindset is a journey, not a proclamation" (p. 2). Viewing the mindset paradigm through the lens of Polyvagal Theory, we come to understand that the path to a growth mindset is a shared journey in relationship with others. Co-regulating with another who holds a growth mindset on our behalf makes it possible to share their belief until we believe it for ourselves.

By now, you're comfortable with the Autonomic Ladder as the metaphor for your nervous system hierarchy of states. Let's view success-oriented, failure-avoidant, and failure-accepting students through a polyvagal lens and create a working model based on traits described in Martin's Wheel. We'll add mindsets to the model and design a visual depicting ANS states and their relationship to the Polyvagal Learning Hub (Figure 6.2).

A growth mindset thrives in a regulated ventral vagal state. The ventral vagal state is associated with characteristics of success-oriented students with positive motivation and engagement (the upper part of the Martin Wheel). Students are more resilient, adaptable, and flexible. Being academically buoyant, success-oriented students bounce back from daily setbacks by adjusting their thinking and utilizing different approaches when they experience challenges. The evolving mindset now becomes a flexible growth mindset, meaning that teachers and students can move in and out of nervous system states with flexibility and remain academically buoyant throughout a learning episode.

From a sympathetic state, students can move into ventral or dorsal vagal. The up or down movement depends on available resources, visually represented by the arrows on the left and right sides of the ANS states.

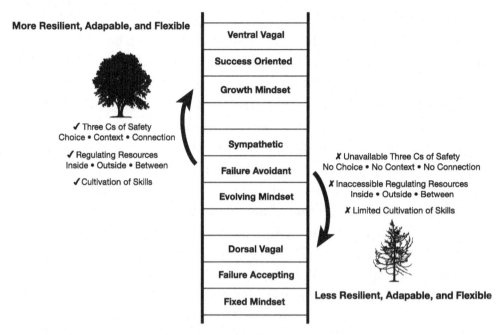

FIGURE 6.2   THE ACADEMIC REGULATION MODEL (Adapted from THE POLYVAGAL THEORY IN THERAPY: ENGAGING THE RHYTHM OF REGULATION by Deb Dana. Copyright © 2018 by Deb Dana. Used by permission of W. W. Norton & Company, Inc.)

The middle is where opportunity lies to harness the disorganized, mobilized sympathetic energy of anxiety, fight, or flight. Learners move toward ventral by accessing ventral resources, increasing feelings of safety, connecting with others, establishing regulation through co-regulation, and continuing to learn essential skills.

Teachers and support staff who model ventral behaviors, including optimism, buoyancy, growth mindsets, and success-oriented characteristics, provide a roadmap for students to find their way to a ventral learning state. A common phrase I use is, "Instead of *telling* children to focus, teach them *how* to focus. Talk less. Show more." We show more by demonstrating buoyant qualities and essential skills we want our students to master.

Without our modeling, support, and resources, failure-avoidant students may be most comfortable staying in a sympathetic state, or they may move down into dorsal vagal. In dorsal vagal, they become failure accepting and exhibit a fixed mindset along with the dorsal vagal emotions of shutting down, disconnection, and disengagement. They transition from wanting to learn to not wanting to learn because it's become too difficult and frustrating. They stay in their comfort zone, unable to generate the motivation and organized mobilizing energy to move through sympathetic and eventually to ventral vagal. In dorsal vagal, students are less resilient, adaptable, and flexible. But they can stay in dorsal vagal and evolve their mindset toward growth when we integrate the Polyvagal Learning Hub with excellent teaching focusing on essential skills.

Until students have the capacity to recognize nervous system state changes and become more academically buoyant, we need to bring our own regulated nervous systems and growth mindsets to our students' learning experiences—holding that space on their behalf. As we befriend our nervous systems and evolve our mindsets, the students learn from our example.

To create environments that nourish growth mindsets, however, we need to expand the way we perceive the brain, starting with changing the metaphor. Paul (2021) writes, "As long as we settle for thinking inside the brain, we'll remain bound by the limits of that organ. But when we reach outside it with intention and skill, our thinking can be transformed" (p. xiii).

The brain is relational and works optimally when accessing available interconnected and interactive resources from inside and outside the body. And we must provide those resources and explicitly teach the brain how to access them. If not, the brain, through grit, effort, and a lot of energy expenditure, will carry on with its burdensome load, but at what cost? Exhaustion. Burnout. Fogginess. Overwhelm. Despair. This is true for us as well as for our students. Like an overloaded washing machine, the heavy load disrupts the brain's rhythmic nature, creating a clunky, out-of-rhythm response and expending more energy to get the job done than if we'd just split the loads into more manageable parts. This is the essence of cognitive load theory—reducing the load so that more energy is available for learning.

Cognitive Load Theory

Cognitive load theory explains the relationship between working memory and long-term memory. While we're actively learning, we use working memory. The ability to recall and utilize information in the future requires transferring the information to long-term memory. The working memory of the brain is limited to five to seven chunks of information. When the working memory is overloaded, then only a limited amount of information gets sent to long-term memory (Hawthorne et al., 2019).

Students with overloaded working memories have a difficult time with skills common to success-oriented students, including planning, remembering, and focusing (Shay & Pohan, 2021). Come time to recall what's learned, there may be little to nothing stored in long-term memory.

Trauma, anxiety, and negative emotions add to cognitive load because they make it difficult to access higher cognitive functions (Perry & Winfrey, 2021). A student's well-being influences learning and reduces the cognitive load on working memory (Hawthorne et al., 2019). If we want students to be ventral learners, reducing cognitive load is an important objective. Motivation and engagement increase with reduced cognitive load (Martin, 2016).

While there are effective strategies designed to reduce cognitive load during learning episodes, including Load Reduction Instruction and the I Do, We Do, You Do Model (Martin & Evans, 2018), there are additional ways to reduce cognitive load that align with Polyvagal Theory.

The Three Types of Cognition

Cognition takes many forms. The formal names for the three main types of cognition are *embodied cognition*, *situated cognition*, and *distributed cognition* (Paul, 2021). Within classroom environments, it's important to elevate these three types of cognition and integrate them into learning frameworks. By doing so, there's an opportunity to expand the view of resilience that's frequently associated with the brain-based resolve of grit and effort. Understanding that intelligence and thinking well aren't about working the brain harder pushes us out of our "mind as muscle" comfort zones. We optimize the phrase "work harder, not smarter" by using extended ventral resources inside our bodies (embodied cognition), in the environment (situated cognition), and shared within relationships between others (distributed cognition).

Inside: Embodied Cognition

Embodied cognition research supports the notion that cognition is affected by states in the body and that there are resources within us, beyond the brain, that are available to solve problems (Wilson & Golonka, 2013). Embodied cognition is a broad area of study. Within the application of Polyvagal Theory, this discussion is limited to three resources: naming states of the ANS, interoceptive awareness, and gesturing.

Naming states of the nervous system is proven by research to reduce activity in the amygdala, the area of the brain responsible for processing fear and other strong emotions (Javanbackht & Saab, 2017). When we bring awareness to our nervous system states and name them, this reduces the impact of those emotions. Through awareness, we're more readily able to seek ways to address those emotions such as accessing ventral resources, noticing micromoments of ventral energy, or reaching out to others for support. When states are named and addressed, there's more access to higher-level cognitive functioning like problem solving (Perry & Winfrey, 2021). As you've learned, the ability to name nervous system states requires good interoceptive awareness.

The interoceptive sense is an embodied cognitive resource. Researchers measure interoception by the heartbeat detection test. Those with better interoceptive awareness are more readily able to detect their own heart rates. Current research on heart rate variability is showing that improving our interoceptive awareness has numerous benefits, including being more resilient (Sha'ari & Amin, 2021). Those with better interoception can make sounder decisions, be more buoyant academically, and bring greater insights into their relationships with others. Mindfulness and meditative practices hone interoceptive awareness. There are also specific strategies, too involved to list here, that can be taught to help children improve interoceptive awareness (Mahler, 2017).

While feelings of safety and danger register inside us through interoception, signals from others affect our sense of safety as well. Though it's common knowledge that we read body language to detect expressions of safety and danger, hand gesturing can be used during learning episodes to increase feelings of safety and reduce cognitive load.

Hand gesturing assists with prosody of speech, increases understanding when used to illustrate key points, and contributes to grasping abstract concepts (Paul, 2021; Shattuck-Hufnagel & Ren, 2018). Gesturing supports the Social Engagement System, adding another layer of communication between people in relationships. It's easier to learn new concepts when gesturing accompanies verbal instructions or information. Notice students in your classroom who gesture versus those who don't. The ones who gesture may have better comprehension skills. Encourage students to make meaningful hand gestures to illustrate key points they want other students to remember. When you're teaching, be sure to gesture as well. For instance, when you're teaching students about the three states of the nervous system, physically step to the right each time you name a different state. Next, have your students stand, move with you, gesture, and repeat the three states along with you. Last, ask your students to partner with another student and go through the gesturing exercise. The mind is now able to use the added embodied resource of gesturing to remember the three states of the nervous system.

When adding movement to gesturing or any other learning activity, this is an additional example of embodied cognition that leads to improved understanding of concepts (Toumpaniari et al., 2015). In classrooms, we've long known that children learn better when learning is linked to movement. Using the body to learn is no longer an aside or a quick five minutes following along with a movement video. The evidence is strong and clear. The outdated notion that we have a thought and then move our bodies has been updated through science. We now know that moving our bodies influences our thoughts and improves thinking, memory retention, and memory recall (Paul, 2021). Students work smarter, not harder, by moving their bodies and gesturing during learning activities. Once we've applied the important concepts of embodied cognition, we continue to lighten cognitive load by using resources in the environment.

Outside: Situated Cognition

Scientists who study situated cognition focus on the how the environment affects learning. Deb Dana's Three Cs of Safety (context, choice, and connection) are examples of situated cognition. Learning is contextual, relating to our sense of safety, belonging, and control over the environment.

In the classroom, the application of situated cognition can be as easy as creating a nature place in the room where children go to experience the stress-reducing qualities of natural environments. Taking a break and walking around the campus while noticing plants, birds, and cloud formations is an example of using situated cognition to refresh the mind.

Allowing children to help arrange the classroom and create their own personal spaces is another way to increase their sense of belonging and tap into those resources outside of themselves. Students having control over where they sit and how they arrange their personal space increases their sense of safety.

Think about when you go to a conference. If you've gone with a friend, your comfort level is already higher than if you attended by yourself. Alone, you'll look around and take in the room through activation of your senses. Neuroception and interoception provide information coming in from your body, and help you choose a place to sit that feels safe. This might be by the nearest door just in case the lecture is a snooze-fest and you want to exit stage left without being seen. If you know the speaker and enjoy the topic, you may sit closer to the front where you can engage more easily with the speaker and others in the room.

Once you've found your comfortable, safe spot, you'll sit there consistently throughout the day. If the speaker asks everyone to move to a new spot to meet new people, a noticeable collective sigh of discontent rumbles through the room. Now everyone must figure out how to feel safe again. That's a lot of cognitive load on the brain. You can bet if you're one of the ones who didn't want to move, your ability to learn new information is momentarily paused until your sense of safety comes back online.

There's no difference between your students attending your class on the first day and you attending day one of a conference. Choice is a powerful example of increasing safety under the umbrella of situated cognition.

Creating workspaces that provide options for learning including quiet spaces, places with headphones and calming music, standing desk options, seated floor cushions, rocking chairs, group seating, and individual seating lighten the cognitive load by providing resources that increase comfort and promote safety in the environment.

Have supplies available so students can move their thinking from inside their brains to outside in the environment. Note pads, markers, highlighters, individual white boards, chart paper for creating graphic organizers, and manipulatives are examples of extending the mind into the environment. The brain's working memory gets a break and doesn't have to hold onto all that information.

One of the most cognitive load-bearing issues in classrooms today is time or lack thereof. This is true for teachers who constantly experience a lack of time to cover the broad curricula along with students who don't have enough time to learn the material. Time is a situated resource that some students must have to reduce their cognitive load and learn with ease.

Teachers and support staff reveal "not enough time" as one of their most pressing issues affecting their work environment and their ability to collaborate successfully with others (Wilson, 2015). Teachers experience emotional exhaustion, health issues, and excessive stress due to work-related time pressure (Maas et al., 2021). There are no easy answers to the time pressure teachers and students feel in today's fast-paced classrooms. However, social support from the school principal can reduce the perception of time pressure and emotional exhaustion (Maas et al., 2021).

Though we can't magically fix the time issues, we can bring awareness to the feelings within us associated with time pressure. When those feeling emerge, taking a micromoment to reset with a deep sigh and finding a glimmer of ventral energy in our environment nourishes the nervous system. With time being something there's just not enough of these days, thinking of time in terms of micromoments may help reduce time-related fatigue.

Through utilizing embodied and situated cognition resources, you and your students are well on the way to finding a rhythm in the classroom that helps everyone evolve their mindsets toward growth. Let's repurpose the phrase "many hands make light work" to remember the third and final type of cognition, where we lighten the cognitive load by sharing it with others.

Between: Distributed Cognition

The science of distributed cognition focuses on learning shared with others through working collaboratively in teams and optimizing group think. Through the lens of distributed cognition, learning is a shared journey that is enhanced by relationships with others—a polyvagal anthem.

Types of distributed cognition in classrooms include activities where students move together in synchrony, work out problems in teams, and create projects in groups. The essence of distributed cognition is capitalizing on collective intelligence (Riedl et al., 2021). Together students can learn more, do more, and create more when working together than when working in isolation.

To prepare students to embrace group thinking and working collaboratively, create a class ritual that includes synchronized movement provides the glue that bonds students to one another—a collective caring. Following along while watching movement on a screen, popular in classrooms, is not the type of synchrony that promotes group synergy. Students need to move together while looking at one another, not while looking at a screen. With increased online learning, synchronized movement is still possible if students are looking at each other on-screen rather than following along individually while watching a video.

With the establishment of group, synchronized movement activity, students are primed to shift from individual thinking to shared thinking with other students. Moving together with others sends a signal that we are able and willing to work and learn cooperatively (Rabinowitch & Meltzoff, 2017).

Distributed cognition can be seen as a nourishing exercise for the nervous system. Working together, co-regulating with others, finding ways to make learning playful, and creating meaningful relationships are the nectar of Polyvagal Theory for teachers, staff, and students alike.

Be sure students have access to the ventral resources in the Polyvagal Learning Hub and are aware of their nervous system states during group activities. Your introvert students may need different resources than your extrovert students. Design group activities so students discover roles within the group that keep them in a place of ventral learning.

Reducing cognitive load and fertilizing growth mindsets begins with understanding that cognition takes many forms, and within those forms lies a deep well of resources to support student learning. Ensuring students know how to access resources paves the path to ventral learning—the kind of learning that keeps students flexibly able to adapt to daily classroom challenges.

Cognitive Flexibility

Cognitive flexibility is a high-ranking predictor of resilience and being able to think divergently to adapt to an ever-changing world (Buttelmann & Karbach, 2017). Cognitive flexibility is defined as the ability to switch between tasks, control actions, and adapt flexibly to environments (Braem & Egner, 2018; Buttelmann & Karbach, 2017).

According to Yavuz and Kutlu (2016), students with a high level of cognitive flexibility find solutions for problems and believe success is possible provided they apply grit and make enough effort. Shifting to an evolving mindset and extended mind perspective, we come to understand that student achievement relies less on grit and effort and more on reducing cognitive load. Reducing cognitive load creates space for more cognitive flexibility. For example, when you cram a bunch of books and papers into an overstuffed box, there's no flexibility or room in the box to organize the information neatly. If you reduce the amount of books and paper in the box, you create space with more flexible options for organizing the material—finding the best solution to meet the organizing objective.

Cognitive flexibility is an important aspect of adaptability, allowing us to adjust our thoughts, switch gears, discover new perspectives, and become ventral learners. Cognitive flexibility is shown to be a significant predictor of reading and math skills in a meta-analysis focusing on students ages four to 13 (Buttelmann & Karbach, 2017). Studies also align cognitive flexibility with emotional regulation, including mood and anxiety challenges (Gabrys et al., 2018). Within the context of stressful situations, cognitive flexibility "might be expressed through the ability to effectively regulate, or disengage from, negative thoughts and emotions when they no longer serve an adaptive purpose" (Gabrys et al., 2018, p. 3).

The ability to effectively regulate and disengage from negative thoughts and emotions relies on befriending the nervous system. A flexible nervous system can adjust and adapt to ever-changing situations and lays the foundation for a flexible cognitive system to do the same.

Let's put everything we've learned on our journey thus far into a metaphorical backpack. This lovely metaphor serves to illustrate how we now have the resources to travel the ventral learning path and share the experience with others.

The Ventral Path to Joyful Learning

Think about heading out for a day's hike with a backpack stuffed with water, snacks, bug spray, first aid supplies, map, compass, rain gear, and a flashlight. Your backpack, with its essentials, increases your adaptability. You're prepared for a change in weather, a scraped knee, or pesky mosquitos.

Now think of ventral resources as your backpack on the path to joyful learning. In this backpack are your lightweight ventral anchors, your glimmers of ventral energy, your understanding of the reparative continuum, your safety rest stops, and all the other skills you've learned so far in this book. Your ventral backpack can be carried with you into any situation.

As these polyvagal concepts are learned by others, they'll join you on your ventral path, stepping alongside you with their backpacks filled with their own ventral resources. If someone runs out of snacks, others can offer their snacks. When in need of a glimmer, there are glimmers to share. When your backpack gets too heavy, your companion offers to carry some of the heavier items for you.

With any journey there are mishaps. In our backpacks is the reparative continuum. We find our way back from disconnection to connection through the reparative process. When lost, we provide safety rest stops, a place to pause and discover new paths forward.

Imagine classrooms, where everyone (teachers, support staff, and students alike) carries a ventral backpack, ready to share with one another on this earthly path we're hiking together. We're able to take in through our senses the beauty of nature and feel the energy move within us. We give our busy minds a rest, take a deep breath, and bring awareness to the moments of microconnections and collective caring we discover along the way. That's the incredibly hopeful experience of being on the polyvagal path to joyful learning.

REFLECTING ON WHAT YOU'VE LEARNED

- When viewing mindsets, there's a continuum between fixed and growth that is dependent on context, cognitive story, and nervous system state at the time of the learning event. This is described as an evolving mindset because it's fluid and flexible, with any place within the cycle being accepted and supported.

- Mindsets and the three types of learners on Martin's Wheel are integrated into the Academic Learning Model. You're able to see at a glance how the Polyvagal Learning Hub resources can help students become regulated, success-oriented learners. Conversely, without the learning hub resources, students may continue the cycle of failure. In the middle of the model is the critical junction between success and failure. Which students in your class are stuck in the middle? What resources can you provide to support their movement toward ventral vagal?

- Cognitive load theory focuses on working memory and its relationship to long-term memory. When working memory is overloaded, there's limited transfer of information to long-term memory. Reducing cognitive load is essential for ventral learning. Have you experienced cognitive overload recently? What are some ways you could lighten your load?

- There are three types of cognition: embodied, situated, and distributed. Each type of cognition is a valuable resource that reduces cognitive load. Do students in your classroom know where to find additional cognitive resources when needed? What types of resources can they access?

- Cognitive flexibility is related to resilience and adaptability. Nervous system flexibility is an important precursor to cognitive flexibility. In what ways do you stretch your students' nervous systems and cognitive systems without creating additional cognitive load?

APPLYING WHAT YOU'VE LEARNED

ACTIVITY ONE: Exploring Your Evolving Mindset

When you're experiencing a situation that stretches your skills or abilities, notice where you're landing on the mindset cycle. Is your mindset growth, fixed, or evolving? If fixed or evolving, what does your nervous system need to move you into a growth mindset? Being able to observe your nervous system state and your mindset at the same time takes practice, but you'll eventually master the art of an evolving mindset—where any place in the cycle is an opportunity for curiosity and exploration.

ACTIVITY TWO: Reviewing Staff Adaptability and Flexibility

During these turbulent times in education, how adaptable and flexible are you and your staff? In terms of the ventral path, where do your staff members spend most of their time during staff meetings? Do you notice a correlation between mindsets and nervous system states? What activity could you share with your staff to support growth mindsets and increase ventral energy for those whose ventral energy is running low?

ACTIVITY THREE: Observing One Student's Mindset

During learning events, observe one student and begin the process of recognizing when you need to hold a space for a growth mindset on the student's behalf. Verbally express that you believe in their ability to learn the material. Together with the student, discover cognitive load-reducing resources that help the student bring their thinking out into the environment. Explicitly teach the student how to access these newly discovered resources when needed.

ACTIVITY FOUR: Charting the Three Types of Cognition in Your Classroom

On a piece of paper, create three columns. Write the words *embodied,* *situated,* and *distributed* as headings. List the strategies, activities, items, and spaces in your classroom that qualify under each of those headings. You may need to look back at this section in the chapter to review each of the three types of cognition.

How effectively are you utilizing the resources within each cognition category? Do students know how to access the resources? Are there gaps where you could create more resources and reduce cognitive load for your students?

CHAPTER 7

The Seven Polyvagal Principles for the Classroom

Students with just about every label found their way into the class-room of my friend and colleague, Ms. D. It was beautiful, complete with artistically stenciled cabinets, habitats housing an array of critters, and plants growing beyond their potted boundaries. Like her plants, the students under her tutelage grew beyond their boundaries as well.

She often invited me into her classroom to try out new activities with her students. On one of our give-it-a-try days, we were integrating a series of reading-movement activities into their literacy lessons. I subscribe to the adage, "you teach best what you most need to learn" (Bach, 1977). After a general introduction, the second-grade students engaged for two hours, taking turns teaching one another the new activities and then designing their own versions. Before the final bell, with 20 minutes to spare, a student known for being extremely hyperactive raised his hand and asked, "Ms. D., can we just read now?"

All the activities of the day provided his nervous system with lots of opportunity to organize his disorganized, mobilized energy. This student, rarely in his seat, was finally ready to just sit and read, his satiated nervous system yearning for a quieting experience.

Ms. D.'s reputation for drawing everything wonderful out of students made most parents ask for her by name. The reward for her success? A room full of complex, diverse students in need of nervous system befriending. Undeterred, she discovered unique strengths in every student, made learning meaningful, and created an environment with engagement at its core. Ms. D. managed to bring every student into the light of her unbridled love for all humans within her sphere of influence. Though she didn't know the specific language of Polyvagal Theory, Ms. D. spoke it like a native.

On our polyvagal journey, we've covered a lot of miles. You may feel like a visitor learning to speak a new language in a foreign country. Chances are you speak more polyvagal than you realize. You'll find the concepts we've discussed integrate beautifully with your ways of knowing the world.

For instance, looking through the lens of trauma-informed practice, the Polyvagal Learning Hub integrates well with the Wheel of Awareness that focuses on mindful attention practices using eight senses (Jennings, 2019a; Siegel, 2009).

If your lens is a social–emotional learning (SEL) perspective, the Polyvagal Learning Hub fits into the center portion of the Core SEL Competencies (McKown, 2019). For students to achieve the SEL competencies, they need access to the resources found in the Polyvagal Learning Hub (Figure 5.3).

Teaching students how to befriend their nervous systems complements any strategies implemented through a sensory-based, neurodevelopmental lens. As an example, within a colored zone approach, behavior is aligned with particular zones, and students are taught to recognize their colored zones (Chaves & Taylor, 2021; Delahooke, 2019; Kuypers, 2011). Integrating the befriending process and the Hub supports these approaches. Applying Polyvagal Theory adds a deeper layer of understanding when students are taught to observe and name nervous system states related to the colored zones.

Through Polyvagal Theory we understand that teachers, support staff, and students move in and out of nervous system states or zones throughout the day. The expectation changes from being in the right zone or state to understanding that we naturally move in and out of regulation throughout the day, depending on signals of safety and danger, as well as experiencing connection and disconnection. Specific behaviors may be an adaptive response that's essential for dealing with a particular situation. The key is to be able to access the resources to move back into a ventral state after the threat has passed or has been ameliorated.

A growing number of practitioners in a variety of fields explain behavior and design treatment protocols using a hierarchal, brain-based neurosequential lens (Barfield et al., 2014; De Luna & Wang, 2021; Erickson & Harvey, 2021; Perry, 2006). Polyvagal Theory integrates with sequential brain and learning models by offering a deeper understanding of the autonomic nervous system's states and their effects on the brain. As you've learned, the brain and the ANS are intimately connected and affected by each other. The more we understand their symbiotic relationship, the better we'll be at designing environments that support a variety of neurodiverse learners.

Regardless of the lens you choose to look through, the polyvagal principles covered in each of these chapters are useful in guiding your professional practice and producing positive outcomes for staff and students alike (Collie et al., 2020). The joyful path to learning begins with bringing each of the seven principles into your classroom and weaving them into what you already do—using the lens that feels safe and comfortable for you.

Getting Started With the Seven Polyvagal Principles

The mantra of this book is, *you go first*. While you may want to start right away with your students, be sure you've internalized the seven polyvagal principles for yourself.

As the befriending process evolves, our Autonomic Ladder becomes alive, flexible, and fluid. There's a flow as we move in and out of our nervous system states, becoming a polyvagal dance that pirouettes within us—a relational dance of connection with ourselves and others. It's in this place that we find safety and refuge—moments in time to rest, reset, and reframe the events of the day. In doing so, we're able to see the world and our work from the vantage point of hope and optimism exemplified by the words of Emily Dickinson: "I dwell in Possibility . . . The spreading wide my narrow Hands / To gather Paradise." This brings us to the final, seventh polyvagal principle.

> ### *PRINCIPLE SEVEN: Dwell in possibility and an enormous amount of curiosity.*

Now let's review all the principles, complete with bullet points to punctuate simple ways to bring them to life.

PRINCIPLE ONE: *Befriend your nervous system.*
- Be patient with yourself.
- Celebrate the small steps toward befriending your nervous system.
- Observe and name your states as you move out of regulation and back into regulation.

PRINCIPLE TWO: *Safety and connection lead to motivation and engagement.*
- Begin using CLA to bring awareness to the layers that create your narratives.
- Notice how feeling safe or unsafe affects your bodily sensations and ability to focus, attend, and engage with the task at hand.
- When feeling unsafe, ask yourself, "Is this an appropriate response in this moment?"

PRINCIPLE THREE: *Co-regulation comes before self-regulation.*
- Know that when you're dysregulated, you can tap into regulating resources inside yourself, outside in your environment, and through relationships with others.
- When feeling dysregulated, ask yourself, "In this moment, what does my nervous system need?"
- When you take care of your nervous system's needs, you're able to share your regulated nervous system with others in need.

PRINCIPLE FOUR: *Resilience develops through retuning the nervous system.*
- Notice when feelings of disconnection happen between yourself and someone else. Tend to the "miss" in order to mend the "miss."
- Discord is healthy and stretches the nervous system when both people can bring ventral resources to the discussion. Be aware of

your nervous system state during times of discord and attempt to keep ventral in view.

- Look for glimmers in the micromoments of your day and discover opportunities to share microconnections with others.

PRINCIPLE FIVE: *Adaptability relies on access to ventral resources.*

- Refer to your list of your ventral vagal resources when you notice yourself moving into sympathetic or dorsal vagal states.
- Your regulating resources may change depending on the situation and phase of your life. Add or remove resources from your ventral backpack as needed.
- When you visit your go-to place within, notice what ventral resources bring you back to your regulated place of safety and connection.

PRINCIPLE SIX: *Nervous system flexibility underpins cognitive flexibility.*

- Lighten your cognitive load by utilizing resources in your environment that support memory by writing lists, drawing pictures, or using a daily electronic or hard copy planner. Organize or categorize information by using colored markers, colored index cards, or highlighters.
- When tackling something new, observe your mindset and utilize ventral resources to evolve your mindset toward growth.
- Welcome new experiences or challenges as opportunities to expand your nervous system's capacity to stretch, while remaining regulated.

PRINCIPLE SEVEN: *Dwell in possibility and an enormous amount of curiosity.*

- When you're frustrated with yourself for being unable to do something that's important to you, consider the possibility that you just haven't figured it out yet, and you will.
- Take a break and throw yourself into something enjoyable when struggling with a decision or taxing situation. Let your mind come out and play.
- Dysregulation is an opportunity to be curious about what's triggering you. Rather than judging or being hard on yourself, be curious.

Ask yourself, "I'm curious why I became dysregulated during that situation. What could I do next time to remain regulated?"

These principles are my own interpretation of polyvagal concepts. They are a starting place to begin an interdisciplinary conversation with friends and colleagues. May they light a polyvagal campfire that calls us to gather around and share our stories, perspectives, insights, and wisdom. Within the crackles and pops, the light and shadows, we hear and see universal truths that bring us together in our oneness, our humanity on this planet.

Becoming Fluent in Polyvagal

Using polyvagal vocabulary, we're now able to understand ourselves and others through the language of the nervous system. We started walking the polyvagal path together with a brief introduction setting the stage for exploring why the concepts of Polyvagal Theory are worth our time. At the root of polyvagal-guided teaching is the essential concept of the befriending process. We need to befriend our own nervous systems before expecting others around us to befriend theirs. Befriending from within creates the synergy to befriend the nervous systems around us—one nervous system to another.

By understanding the three states of the autonomic nervous system, we come to understand the associated stories that accompany each state. Through the ventral vagal state, we see the world as an inviting and welcoming place. Through the sympathetic state, we experience a world that feels unsafe and uninviting, causing us to want to fight or flee. In the dorsal vagal state, the world is not safe enough to be in it, and we withdraw into an immobilized place of isolation. Knowing how to tap into ventral resources is an important aspect of the befriending process and being able to find our way back up to ventral vagal—back to a place of hope and possibility.

We have a biological need for safety, connection, and co-regulation. The safety scale is a metaphor that describes how feelings of safety and danger interact with one another. When feeling unsafe, we need to recognize those nudges and find resources that help create an environment from within us and outside us where we feel safe enough to engage with all life has to offer—the ups, the downs, the twists and turns.

Through the reparative continuum, we've learned how to recon-nect after we disconnect from ourselves or others due to feeling unsafe, unseen, or dysregulated. The continuum visually represents the depth of disconnection, from miss and mend, to rupture and repair, to breach and build. We may need additional mental health resources and support to reconnect with ourselves, others, and the world depending on where a disconnecting event lands on the continuum.

We are the cartographers of our danger maps, influenced by our life experiences. Along our journey, when experiencing danger zones, we're able to reconnect with the resources within us to reset through utilizing safety rest stops—momentary pauses that bring ventral energy back into our nervous system.

Through ventral vagal anchors, we access regulating resources when visiting our nervous system's go-to place within. Throughout the day, we move with flexibility in and out of different states, knowing that we have a path back to ventral through our regulating resources. We expand our resilience and adaptability by leaning into the opportunities that stretch our nervous system's comfort zone. By bringing awareness to our states, we're able to observe and name them. This takes the mystery out of why we react as we do to different triggers. Taking moments to find glimmers around us helps keep ventral in view. We're learning how to listen within.

Dwelling in possibility and curiosity requires additional knowledge about how our nervous systems and brains are wired to engage with the world. Dr. Iain McGilchrist (2018) authored *The Master and His Emissary: The Divided Brain and the Making of the Western World*. His 500-page, small-print book focuses on the differences between the two hemispheres of the brain. His extensive review of the literature and research expands our understanding of the split brain and clarifies the continual debates about hemisphere specialization. McGilchrist (2018) states,

> *When people object that each hemisphere is involved in every-thing we do, they are right. When they assume that means there are no differences, they are wrong. It is not what each hemisphere does, but how it does it that matters. Each hemisphere is involved in everything, true enough; just in a quite different way.* (p. x)

The Divided Brain on a Hike

Let's bring this divided brain understanding to life by revisiting the back-pack metaphor from Chapter 6. The right hemisphere is excited to start the journey. It's interested in all the options of where the journey may lead, the sights and sounds, the rich sensory stimulation along the path, and meeting unexpected visitors during the hike.

The left hemisphere, on the other hand, wants to make sure your back-pack is filled with essentials for the trip. It wants to know the starting and end points, how long it will take, where to find the mile markers, and the objective for taking the hike in the first place.

The left hemisphere is a closed-loop system, and the right hemisphere is an open-loop system (McGilchrist, 2018). The left hemisphere looks within itself to find facts, patterns, and truths. The right hemisphere reaches out in relationship with others and lives in expectant anticipation of what's new to come.

The right hemisphere loves to dwell in possibility and curiosity. The left hemisphere wants to reign in the concept of possibility and curiosity so it can identify, categorize, and integrate incoming information with schemes already created. The left hemisphere wants to set limits and create boundaries around how much possibility you should dwell in and how curious you ought to be.

The Two Hemispheres of Education

I often hear professionals outside the education field lament the slow rate of progress toward an educational system that values creative humans in the classroom as much as it values graphs, percentiles, and bell curves. Once again, we turn to the phenomenon of the divided brain for insight.

Education policies, trends, and mandates reflect the biases inherent in the two hemispheres of the brain. Dr. Ulcca Joshi Hansen, in her book, *The Future of Smart,* clearly synthesized important elements of McGilchrist's research into this one succinct paragraph:

> *Our comprehension of the world begins in the right hemisphere, with input from the senses [the nervous system]. That data is*

then passed to the left hemisphere for technical functions like analysis, measurement, and codification, especially through language. Information is then passed back to the right hemisphere for a full synthesis—an integration of our experience at all levels that leads to decisions and action. (Hansen, 2021, p. 43)

All learning begins in the nervous system pathways. The sensory information is sent up to the right hemisphere where engagement begins. All too often, we dismiss the wants and needs of the right hemisphere by passing out worksheets. This satisfies the left hemisphere but can leave the right hemisphere feeling like it's missing out on the party. The expression, "You can lead a horse to water, but you can't make it drink" is often a mantra for teachers who are disappointed in students' lack of enthusiasm for learning. However, without involvement from the right hemisphere, the odds are high that those students won't have an insatiable thirst for learning. It's the mind–body–world connection that brings Polyvagal Theory alive in our classrooms. The right hemisphere loves the novel, sensory-rich experiences of connecting in the world, connecting to one another, and connecting to the material being taught. To extend the metaphor, you may need to lead the horse to water by making it thirsty and salting its oats. We salt the oats by creating learning spaces that promote curiosity, engage the senses, and light up the right hemisphere.

McGilchrist (2018) makes a solid argument that the Western world is left hemisphere biased. We need to shift from the Western world's left-brain bias of measuring, categorizing, enumerating, and standardizing learning and make a right-brain shift that encourages teachers' and students' minds to come out and play. Instead of cramming stuff into students, let's draw wonderful stuff out. It's in the cramming, the fast-paced delivery of curricula, and the constant measuring that we're getting hung up.

The left hemisphere of education finds comfort in simplifying the complex and creating systems that can be measured, quantified, and compared. We end up teaching only that which is easy to measure. The right hemisphere of education is concerned with the human aspects of relationships, belonging, sharing, and learning through experience—much more difficult to measure but important all the same. We lean to the left because it feels safer. Until we find ways to move to the right safely, we'll keep returning to the comforts of the simplified, measured left.

Is there a way to build a bridge between the right and left for safe crossing? A little more neuroscience explains what needs to happen next to bring the divided brain of education into a cohesive whole.

In the brain, the *corpus callosum* supports communication between the right and left hemispheres and also suppresses information (McGilchrist, 2018). There are some things each hemisphere needs to know and others that are best kept with the confines of each hemisphere's neural ramblings.

We need to find the corpus callosum bridge in education—a way to bring together the needs, wants, and interests of both hemispheres while allowing them to work independently when that is what's best served. Do we need to measure what students are learning? Sure. It's how we measure that makes the difference in motivation and engagement. Personal best goals, performance-based assessments, and portfolios of joy (as one teacher calls her students' portfolios) do far more to nurture growth mindsets and bring ventral energy into the learning experience than do standardized measurements (Dintersmith, 2018; Martin & Elliot, 2015).

The application of Polyvagal Theory in your classroom is not just one more thing to do, implement, or measure. This information is here to support you, live inside you, nurture you. There's no curriculum to implement or checklist to complete (much to the dismay of your left hemisphere).

Teachers across the country are transforming the way they teach and how their students learn by understanding that the magic is in the micro-moments. Those brief sprinkles of joy, glimmers, excitement, curiosity, and connection. It's the cumulative power of moments that transform something ordinary into something extraordinary, including our educational system.

Afterword: Coming Full Circle

Writing this book has been a professional and personal journey for me. I use the concepts discussed within these pages every day in my educational consulting practice along with parenting Shalea. Together, my daughter and I have tried a wide variety of therapeutic interventions. Polyvagal Theory has melded everything together into a cohesive whole. It's brought so much more understanding and joy to our mother–daughter relationship.

Picking up where the preface left off, Shalea entered elementary school, and a wonderful team gathered around her. Each member helped in their own way. We shared the challenging job of teaching Shalea to read and write. Having the reading background, I designed her literacy lessons and sent them to school with her, a week at a time. In order for Shalea to be engaged and motivated, I crafted the materials based on her cognitive strengths and personal interests. She progressed, slow and steady, until reaching a functional reading level.

By age 12, her language, which we had worked so hard to develop, declined from full sentences to short phrases, and then to one-word responses. Visits to medical doctors and specialists yielded possibilities for her loss including apraxia and aphasia; however, the cause for the decline remained uncertain at best. Due to Shalea's loss of language, I registered her for a teen sign language class. After attending the first day, I asked,

"Did you enjoy your class?" Putting together her last fluid sentence, she replied, "It's just easier to talk!"

In high school, Shalea made wonderful friends and loved going to school. She attended her junior–senior prom with a kind young man born without a corpus callosum and thriving all the same. With leg braces peeking out beneath his tux pant legs, and one dance move between them, they danced until the very last song.

Come time to walk across the stage to get her high school diploma, Shalea couldn't bring herself to attend the ceremony. She spent the day at home, crying off and on, in total despair that her high school days were ending. The thought of not being able to see her friends every day was more than her tender heart could bear. Though I looked forward to witnessing this joyous milestone, we ordered her favorite pizza and had a quiet, bittersweet celebration at home.

Shalea communicates by texting—sending frequent messages revealing the depth of emotion and thoughts meandering around that inquisitive mind of hers. A quirky sense of humor shines through between her interesting word choices and accompanying emojis.

For fun, Shalea completes 4,000-piece expert LEGO sets at a dazzling pace and thousand-piece puzzles in no time. She rarely forgets *anything*. Shalea loves helping in the fulfillment center of our family business. Like a typical young adult, she argues with me about how late she should be able to stay up and how long she can play on her technology.

Shalea has incredible strengths and also severe challenges—a large file box holds her medical records, complete with a long list of diagnoses. Autism is a recent addition. What I've learned through understanding Polyvagal Theory is that the diagnosis may be the book title, but the nervous system tells the story. Understanding her behavior through a polyvagal lens, I'm able to ask myself, "In this moment, what does my daughter's nervous system need?" And better still, I'm able to ask myself, "In this moment, what does *my* nervous system need so I can stay regulated and support her?"

Learning to speak the language of polyvagal is the most hopeful and positively impactful thing I've done while on this winding path. In my second book, we'll continue walking the joyful path by focusing on specific classroom activities and strategies to provide additional support with implementing the concepts of this book.

In a perfect world, every school would have a team of counselors, social workers, and mental health specialists fluent in polyvagal language. Until then, may this book provide insights and in some small way offer hope to those in need.

If you're in a situation where life's path has diverted you to places unexpected, know that you're not alone. Celebrate the micromoments of love, glimmers, and connection, rather than looking down the road at the miles to go.

When Shalea was six months old and not meeting any of her developmental milestones, I donated to the local library my copy of *What to Expect the First Year* (Eisenberg et al., 1996). After letting go of the expecting book, I also let go of my own personal expectations as Shalea's mother. This poem emerged from a grieving heart, finding new hope and gratitude for the child who chose me to be her mom.

Expecting
Expecting a child perfect and whole
Expecting
Not expecting a lesson in letting go
Letting go of everything I was expecting
Letting go and embracing
Embracing the moment I said yes
Yes, I expect nothing.
Expecting nothing
Receiving everything
Everything challenging
Everything intriguing
Everything joyful, perfect, and whole
Just as she is
Accepting this moment
Joyful, perfect, and whole
Just as it is

Thank you for coming with me on this journey.

References

Andrade, H. L., Brookhart, S. M., & Yu, E. C. (2021). Classroom assessment as co-regulated learning: A systematic review. *Frontiers in Education, 6*, 1–17. https://doi.org/10.3389/feduc.2021.751168

Bach, R. (1977). *Illusions: The adventures of a reluctant messiah.* New York: Dell.

Badenoch, B. (2018). *The heart of trauma: Healing the embodied brain in the context of relationships.* New York: Norton.

Barfield, S., Dobson, C., Gaskill, R., & Perry, B. D. (2014). Neurosequential model of therapeutics in a therapeutic preschool: Implications for work with children with complex neuropsychiatric problems. *Advanced Generalist: Social Work Research Journal, 1*(2), 64–80. https://soar.wichita .edu/handle/10057/10912

Ben-Eliyahu, A. (2019). Academic emotional learning: A critical component of self-regulated learning in the emotional learning cycle. *Educational Psychologist, 54*(13). https://doi.org/10.1080/00461520.2019 .1582345

Benner, A. D. (2011). Latino adolescents' loneliness, academic performance, and the buffering nature of friendships. *Journal of Youth and Adolescence, 40*(5), 556–567. https://doi.org/10.1007/s10964-010-9561-2

Beri, N., & Kumar, D. (2018). Predictors of academic resilience among students: A meta-analysis. *Journal on Educational Psychology, 11*(4), 37–43. https://doi.org/10.26634/jpsy.11.4.14220

Braem, S., & Egner, T. (2018). Getting a grip on cognitive flexibility. *Current Directions in Psychological Science, 27*(6), 470–476. https://doi.org/10.1177/0963721418787475

Bransen, D., Govaerts, M. J. B., Panadero, E., Sluijsmans, D. M. A., & Driessen, E. W. (2021). Putting self-regulated learning in context: Integrating self-, co-, and socially shared regulation of learning. *Medical Education, 56*(1), 29–36. https://doi.org/10.1111/medu.14566

Bueno, D. (2021). Resilience for lifelong learning and well-being. *IBRO/IBE-UNESCO Science of Learning Briefings.* https://solportal.ibe-unesco.org/articles/resilience-for-lifelong-learning-and-well-being/

Buttelmann, F., & Karbach, J. (2017). Development and plasticity of cognitive flexibility in early and middle childhood. *Frontiers in Psychology, 8,* Article 1040. https://doi.org/10.3389/fpsyg.2017.01040

Cain, S. (2013). *Quiet: The power of introverts in a world that can't stop talking.* New York: Random House.

Chavez, J., & Taylor, A. (2021). *The "why" behind classroom behaviors, preK-5: Integrative strategies for learning, regulation, and relationships.* Thousand Oaks, CA: Corwin.

Chen, A. (2019). *The attachment theory workbook: Powerful tools to promote understanding, increase stability, and build lasting relationships.* Emeryville, CA: Althea.

Collie, R., Guay, F., Martin, A. J., Caldecott-Davis, K. & Granziera, H. (2020). Examining the unique roles of adaptability and buoyancy in teachers' work-related outcomes. *Teachers and Teaching, 26*(3–4), 350–364. https://doi.org/10.1080/13540602.2020.1832063

Côté-Lussier, C., & Fitzpatrick, C. (2016). Feelings of safety at school, socioemotional functioning and classroom engagement. *Journal of Adolescent Health, 58*(5), 543–550. https://doi.org/10.1016/j.jadohealth.2016.01.003

Cozolino, L. (2013). *The social neuroscience of education: Optimizing attachment and learning in the classroom.* New York: Norton.

Dana, D. (2018). *The polyvagal theory in therapy: Engaging the rhythm of regulation.* New York: Norton.

Dana, D. (2021). *Anchored: How to befriend your nervous system using polyvagal theory.* Boulder, CO: Sounds True.

Delahooke, M. (2019). *Beyond behaviors: Using brain science and compassion to understand and solve children's behavioral challenges.* Eau Claire, WI: PESI.

De Luna, J. E., & Wang, D. C. (2021). Child traumatic stress and the sacred: Neurobiologically informed interventions for therapists and parents. *Religions, 12*(3), 163. https://dx.doi.org/10.3390/rel12030163

Denworth, L. (2020). *Friendship: The evolution, biology, and extraordinary power of life's fundamental bond.* New York: Norton.

Dintersmith, T. (2018). *What schools could be: Insights and inspirations from teachers across America.* Princeton, NJ: Princeton University Press.

Dweck, C. (2015). Carol Dweck revisits the "growth mindset." *Education Week, 35*(5), 20–24. https://www.edweek.org/leadership/opinion-carol-dweck-revisits-the-growth-mindset/2015/09

Dweck, C. (2016). *Mindset: The new psychology of success.* New York: Ballantine.

Eisenberg, A., Murkoff, H., & Hathaway, S. (1996). *What to expect the first year.* New York: Workman.

Erickson, M., & Harvey, T. (2021, December 5). A framework for a structured approach for formulating a trauma-informed environment. *Journal of Education.* https://doi.org/10.1177/00220574211046811

Frankel, K. K., Brooks M. D., & Learned, J. E. (2021). A meta-synthesis of qualitative research on reading intervention classes in secondary schools. *Teachers College Record, 123*(8), 31–58. https://doi.org/10.1177/01614681211048624

Freund, A. M., & Hennecke, M. (2015). Self-regulation in adulthood. *International Encyclopedia of the Social and Behavioral Sciences.* https://doi.org/10.1016/B978-0-08-097086-8.26061-3

Frisby, B. N., Hosek, A. M., & Beck, A. (2020). The role of classroom relationships as sources of academic resilience and hope. *Communication Quarterly, 65*(5), 1–17. https://doi.org/10.1080/01463373.2020.1779099

Gabrys, R. L., Tabri, N., Anisman, H., & Matheson, K. (2018, November 9). Cognitive control and flexibility in the context of stress and depressive symptoms: The cognitive control and flexibility questionnaire. *Frontiers in Psychology, 9.* https://www.frontiersin.org/article/10.3389/fpsyg.2018.02219

García-Crespo, F. J., Fernández-Alonso, R., & Muñiz, J. (2021). Academic resilience in European countries: The role of teachers, families, and student profiles. *PloS One, 16*(7), e0253409. https://doi.org/10.1371/journal.pone.0253409

Hadwin, A., & Oshige, M. (2011). Self-regulation, co-regulation, and socially shared regulation: Exploring perspectives of social in self-regulated learning theory. *Teachers College Record, 11*(2), 240–264.

Hansen, U. J. (2021). *The future of smart: How our education system needs to change to help all young people thrive.* York, PA: Capucia.

Hawthorne, B. S., Vella-Brodrick, D. A., & Hattie, J. (2019, October 23). Well-being as a cognitive load reducing agent: A review of the literature. *Frontiers in Education, 4.* https://www.frontiersin.org/article/10.3389/feduc.2019.00121

Howell, J. A., Roberts, L. D., & Mancini, V. O. (2018). Learning analytics messages: Impact of grade, sender, comparative information and message style on student affect and academic resilience. *Computers in Human Behavior, 89,* 8–15. https://doi.org/10.1016/j.chb.2018.07.021

Inayatullah, S. (2014). Causal layered analysis defined. Metafuture. https://www.metafuture.org/causal-layered-analysis-cla-defined-2014/

Inayatullah, S. (2017). *Prospective and strategic foresight toolbox: Causal layered analysis.* Paris: Futuribles International.

Javanbackht, A., & Saab, L. (2017, October 27). What happens in the brain when you feel fear? *Smithsonian Magazine.* https://www.smithsonianmag.com/science-nature/what-happens-brain-feel-fear-180966992/

Jennings, P. (2019a). *Mindfulness in the preK–5 classroom.* New York: Norton.

Jennings, P. (2019b). *The trauma-sensitive classroom: Building resilience with compassionate teaching.* New York: Norton.

Jennings, P. (2021). *Teacher burnout turnaround: Strategies for empowered educators.* New York: Norton.

Kain, K. L., & Terrell, S. J. (2018). *Nurturing resilience: Helping clients move forward from developmental trauma.* Berkeley, CA: North Atlantic.

Keller, G. (2012). *The one thing: The suprisingly simple truth behind extraordinary results.* Austin, TX: Bard.

Kuypers, L. M. (2011). *The zones of regulation: A curriculum designed to foster self-regulation and emotional control.* San Jose, CA: Think Social.

Lacoe, J. (2020). Too scared to learn: The academic consequences of feeling unsafe in the classroom. *Urban Education, 55*(10), 1385–1418. https://doi.org/10.1177/0042085916674059

Liew, J., Cao, Q., Hughes, J. N., & Deutz, M. H. F. (2018). Academic resilience despite early academic adversity: A three-wave longitudinal study on regulation-related resiliency, interpersonal relationships, and achievement in first to third grade. *Early Education and Development, 29*(5), 762–779. https://doi.org/10.1080/10409289.2018 .1429766

Maas, J., Schoch, S., Scholz, U., Rackrow, P., Schüler, J., Wegner, M., & Keller, R. (2021). Teachers' perceived time pressure, emotional exhaustion and the role of social support from the school principal. *Social Psychology of Education, 24*, 441–464. https://doi.org/10.1007/ s11218-020-09605-8

Mackesy, C. (2019). *The boy, the mole, the fox, and the horse.* New York: HarperCollins.

Mahapatra, S. (2019). Smartphone addiction and associated consequences: Role of loneliness and self-regulation. *Behaviour and Information Technology, 38*(8), 833–844. https://doi.org/10.1080/0144929X.2018.1560499

Mahler, K. (2017). *Interoception: The eighth sensory system.* Lenexa, KS: AAPC.

Martin, A. J. (2016). *Using load reduction instruction (LRI) to boost motivation and engagement.* Leicester, UK: British Psychological Society.

Martin, A. J., & Burns, E. C. (2014). Academic buoyancy, resilience, and adaptability in students with ADHD. *ADHD Report, 22*(6), 1–9. https:// doi.org/10.1521/adhd.2014.22.6.1

Martin, A. J., & Elliot, A. J. (2015). The role of personal best (PB) goal setting in students' academic achievement gains. *Learning and Individual Differences, 45*, 222–227. https://doi.org/10.1016/j.lindif.2015.12.014

Martin, A. J., & Evans, P. (2018). Load reduction instruction: Exploring a framework that assesses explicit instruction through to independent learning. *Teaching and Teacher Education, 73*, 203–214. https:// doi.org/10.1016/j.tate.2018.03.018

Martin, A. J., & Marsh, H. W. (2009). Academic resilience and academic buoyancy: Multidimensional and hierarchical conceptual framing of causes, correlates and cognate constructs. *Oxford Review of Education, 35*(3), 353–370. https://doi.org/10.1080/03054980902934639

Martin, A. J., Nejad, H. G., Colmar, S., & Liem, G. A. D. (2013). Adaptability: How students' responses to uncertainty and novelty predict their academic and non-academic outcomes. *Journal of Educational Psychology, 105*(3), 728–746. https://doi.org/10.1037/a0032794

Martin, A. J., Nejad, H. G., Colmar, S., Liem, G. A. D., & Collie, R. (2015). The role of adaptability in promoting control and reducing failure dynamics: A mediation model. *Learning and Individual Differences, 38,* 36–43. https://doi.org/10.1016/j.lindif.2015.02.004

McGilchrist, I. (2018). *The master and his emissary: The divided brain and the making of the Western world.* New Haven, CT: Yale University Press.

McKown, C. (2019). *Assessing students' social and emotional learning.* New York: Norton.

McTigue, E. M., Washburn, E. K., & Liew, J. (2009). Academic resilience and reading: Building successful readers. *Reading Teacher, 62*(5), 422–432. https://doi.org/10.1598/RT.62.5.5

Mega, C., Ronconi, L., & De Beni, R. (2014). What makes a good student? How emotions, self-regulated learning, and motivation contribute to academic achievement. *Journal of Educational Psychology, 106,* 121–131. https://doi.org/10.1037/a0033546

Murthy, V. H. (2020). *Together: The healing power of human connection in a sometimes lonely world.* New York: HarperCollins.

Nadworny, E. (2019, February 13). A high-crime neighborhood makes it harder to show up for school. NPR, https://www.npr .org/2019/02/13/693972661

Nasr, S. J. (2013). No laughing matter: Laughter is good psychiatric medicine.*Current Psychiatry, 12*(8), 20–25. https://www.mdedge .com/psychiatry/article/76797/bipolar-disorder/no-laughing -matter-laughter-good-psychiatric-medicine

Neal, D. (2017, August). Academic resilience and caring adults: The experiences of former foster youth. *Child and Youth Services Review 79,* 242–248. https://doi.org/10.1016/j.childyouth.2017.06.005

Nicoll, W. G. (2014). Developing transformative schools: A resilience-focused paradigm for education. *International Journal of Emotional Education, 6*(1), 47–65. https://eric.ed.gov/?id=EJ1085706

Oxford University Press. (n.d.). *Oxford English dictionary.* Retrieved January 13, 2022, from https://www.oed.com/

Patall, E. A., Cooper, H., & Robinson, J. C. (2008). The effects of choice on intrinsic motivation and related outcomes: A meta-analysis of research findings. *Psychological Bulletin, 134*(2), 270–300. https://doi.org/10.1037/0033-2909.134.2.270

Paul, A. M. (2021). *The extended mind: The power of thinking outside the brain.* New York: Houghton Mifflin Harcourt.

Perry, B. D. (2006). Applying principles of neurodevelopment to clinical work with maltreated and traumatized children: The neurosequential model of therapeutics. In N. B. Webb (Ed.), *Working with traumatized youth in child welfare* (pp. 27–52). New York: Guilford.

Perry, B. D., & Winfrey, O. (2021). *What happened to you? Conversations on trauma, resilience, and healing.* New York: Flatiron.

Porges, S. W. (2017). *The pocket guide to the polyvagal theory: The transformative power of feeling safe.* New York: Norton.

Porges, S. W. (2021). *Polyvagal safety: Attachment, communication, self-regulation.* New York: Norton.

Rabinowitch, T., & Meltzoff, A. N. (2017). Synchronized movement experience enhances peer cooperation in preschool children. *Journal of Experimental Child Psychology, 160*, 21–32. https://dx.doi.org/10.1016/j.jecp.2017.03.001

Rao, P. S., & Krishnamurthy, A. R. (2018). Impact on academic resilience on the scholastic performance of high school students. *Indian Journal of Mental Health, 5*(4), 453.

Riedl, C., Kim, Y. J., Gupta, P., Malone, T. W., & Woolley, A. W. (2021). Quantifying collective intelligence in human groups. *Proceedings of the National Academy of Sciences, 118*(21), e2005737118. https://doi.org/10.1073/pnas.2005737118

Romano, L., Angelini, G., Consiglio, P., & Fiorilli, C. (2021). Academic resilience and engagement in high school students: The mediating role of perceived teacher emotional support. *European Journal of Investigation in Health, Psychology, and Education, 11*(2), 334–344. https://doi.org/10.3390/ejihpe11020025

Sha'ari, N. A. S., & Amin, M. K. M. (2021). Resilience building among university students: A heart rate variability biofeedback study. *IOP Conference Series: Materials Science and Engineering.* https://doi.org/10.1088/1757-899X/1051/1/012015

Shattuck-Hufnagel, S., & Ren, A. (2018). The prosodic characteristics of non-referential co-speech gestures in a sample of academic-lecture-style

speech. *Frontiers in Psychology, 9,* 1–13. https://doi.org/10.3389/fpsyg
.2018.01514

Shay, J. E., & Pohan, C. (2021). Resilient instructional strategies: Helping
students cope and thrive in crisis. *Journal of Microbiology and Biology
Education, 22*(1), 22.1.28. https://doi.org/10.1128/jmbe.v22i1.2405

Siegel, D. J. (2009). *Mindsight: The new science of personal transformation.*
New York: Bantam.

Sparks, S. D. (2013, January 4). Social–emotional needs entwined with
students' learning security. *Education Week.* https://www.edweek
.org/leadership/social-emotional-needs-entwined-with-students
-learning-security/2013/01

Stephens, R. (2016). *The left brain speaks, the right brain laughs: A look at the
neuroscience of innovation and creativity in art, science, and life.* Jersey
City, NJ: Cleis.

Stolinker, B. E., & Lafreniere, K. D. (2015). The influence of perceived
stress, loneliness, and learning burnout on university students' educational experience. *College Student Journal, 49*(1), 146–160, EJ1095547.

Toumpaniari, K., Loyens, S., Mavilidi, M., & Paas, F. (2015). Preschool
children's foreign language vocabulary learning by embodying words
through physical activity and gesturing. *Educational Psychology Review,
27,* 445–456.

Tronick, E., & Gold, C. M. (2020). *The power of discord: Why the ups and
downs of relationships are the secret to building intimacy, resilience, and
trust.* Brunswick, Australia: Scribe.

Voros, J. (2005). A generalised "layered methodology" framework. *Foresight, 7*(2), 28–40. https://doi.org/10.1108/14636680510700094

Wang, S., & Aamodt, S. (2012, September). Play, stress, and the learning
brain. *Cerebrum: The Dana forum on brain science, 12.* https://pubmed
.ncbi.nlm.nih.gov/23447798/

Willard, C. (2016). *Growing up mindful: Essential practices to help children,
teens, and families find balance, calm, and resilience.* Boulder, CO: Sounds
True.

Wilson, A. D., & Golonka, S. (2013). Embodied cognition is not what you
think it is. *Frontiers in Psychology, 4,* 1–13. https://doi.org/10.3389/fpsyg
.2013.00058

Wilson, D. (2015). *Collaboration between general education teachers and occupational therapists in classrooms: A layered analysis of professional practice in the USA* [Doctoral dissertation, University of Southern Queensland]. https://eprints.usq.edu.au/27627/1/DissertationMaster-FINAL-WILSON.pdf

Yavuz, H. Ç., & Kutlu, Ö. (2016). Investigation of the factors affecting the academic resilience of economically disadvantaged high school students. *Education and Science, 41*(186), 1–19. https://doi.org/10.15390/EB.2016.5497

Ye, W., Strietholt, R., & Blomeke, S. (2021). Academic resilience: Underlying norms and validity of definitions. *Educational Assessment, Evaluation and Accountability, 33,* 169–202. https://doi.org.10.1007/s11092-020-09351-7

Zimmerman, B. J. (1990). Self-regulated learning and academic achievement: An overview. *Educational Psychologist, 25*(1), 3–17. https://doi.org/10.1207/s15326985ep2501_2

Index

academic(s)
  safety and, 38–43. *see also* safety-
    academic link
academic achievement
  loneliness impact on, 41–43
academic activities
  nervous system states during, 99–103,
    102*f*
academic buoyancy, 70–71
academic emotion(s)
  ANS states and related, 58, 58*f*
academic emotional learning
  described, 57–58, 57*f*, 58*f*
academic emotional learning phases
  observing emotions during, 60
academic regulation model, 101, 102*f*
academic resilience, 8
  academic buoyancy and, 70–71
  cultivating skills of, 71–74, 73*f*
  Polyvagal Theory and, 69–71
  protective factors supporting, 69–71
acceptance
  failure, 92–93
ACEs scores. *see* Adverse Childhood
    Experiences (ACEs) scores
adaptability
  access to ventral resources in, 78–95,
    119

activities related to, 94–95
anchors leading to, 77–79
described, 79
reflecting on, 93–94
resilience and, 78
of staff, 113
vagal brake and, 80
adaptable
  becoming, 93
adaptable learners, 77–95
  anchors of, 77–79. *see also* adaptability;
    anchor(s)
Adverse Childhood Experiences (ACEs)
    scores, 66
affective inclination
  defined, 57
anchor(s)
  adaptability from, 77–79. *see also*
    adaptability
  ventral. *see* ventral anchor(s)
anchored learners, 77–95. *see also*
    anchor(s)
Andrade, H. L., 55–56
ANS. *see* autonomic nervous system (ANS)
assumptions, perceptions, worldviews layer
  in CLA, 30, 30*f*, 32
attachment
  described, 64

Autonomic Ladder, 117
   in classroom, 20–24
   from dorsal vagal state, 22–23
   hierarchy and, 17–23, 18*f*
   map statements related to, 25
   mindsets and, 101–3, 102*f*
   from sympathetic state, 21–22
   from ventral vagal state, 21
autonomic nervous system (ANS)
   Autonomic Ladder in depicting
      hierarchy of, 17–23, 18*f*
   befriend your, 13–26. *see also* "befriend
      your nervous system"
   described, 5
   impact on learning, 5–6
   Polyvagal Theory focusing on functions
      of, 4–6
   responses of, 5
   states of. *see* autonomic nervous
      system (ANS) state(s)
   subsystems of, 15–17, 15*f*
   updating old model of, 16–17
autonomic nervous system (ANS)
      pathway(s)
   growth mindset origins in, 99
   types of, 17–18, 18*f*. *see also specific
      types*
autonomic nervous system (ANS)
      response(s)
   as states, 18–23, 18*f*. *see also specific
      states, e.g.,* ventral vagal state
autonomic nervous system (ANS)
      state(s)
   academic emotions related to, 58, 58*f*
   cognitive story impact of, 52
   Cognitive Story Loop and, 28, 28*f*
   experiencing, 44
   observing/naming, 25
   view from ventral state, 53–54
avoidance
   failure, 92–93
awareness
   to nervous system states, 105

Badenoch, B., 52–53
"befriend your nervous system," 13–26
   activities related to, 25–26
   described, 118

examples of, 116
patience during process of, 23–24
Polyvagal Theory in, 13–26, 116
reflecting on, 24–25
biological rudeness, 36–37
blended state(s)
   described, 81–82, 81*f*
   freeze response in, 86–87
   learning and, 81–88, 81*f*
   of play, 82
   of quietly failing response, 87–88
   of quietly still, 85–86
   reflecting on, 93–94
bonding
   social, 13–14
brain
   divided, 121, 122
   limits of, 97
   metaphors describing, 97
breach(es), 62*f*, 63–65
   causes of, 64
   on reparative continuum, 62*f*, 63–65
   reparative process for, 63–64
building
   after breaches, 62*f*, 63–65
buoyancy
   academic, 70–71
burned out
   disillusioned vs., 12

care
   self-. *see* self-care
Causal Layered Analysis (CLA), 28–34,
      28*f*, 30*f*
   benefits of using, 29–30
   described, 28–32, 28*f*, 30*f*
   exploring, 44
   layers of, 29–32, 30*f*. *see also* Causal
      Layered Analysis (CLA) layer(s)
   metaphors related to, 33
   narratives and, 28–32, 28*f*, 30*f*
   reconstructing portion of, 32–34
   reflecting on, 44
   transformation related to, 32–34
Causal Layered Analysis (CLA) layer(s),
      29–32, 30*f*
   assumptions, perceptions, worldviews
      layer, 30, 30*f*, 32

myths, metaphors, themes, stories
    layer, 30, 30f, 32–33
observable behavior (litany) layer,
    29–31, 30f
systems layer, 30–31, 30f
central nervous system (CNS)
    described, 14–16, 15f
choice(s)
    ideal number of, 39–40
    safety related to, 34–35, 39–40
CLA. see Causal Layered Analysis (CLA)
classroom(s)
    Autonomic Ladder in, 20–24
    connection opportunities in, 65
    neurodevelopmental interventions in,
        xxii–xxviii
    polyvagal principles for, 115–24
    self-care in, 23–24
    self-kindness in, 23–24
    skills related to application of Polyvagal
        Theory in, 73–74, 73f
CNS. see central nervous system
    (CNS)
co-dysregulation, 51
cognition
    distributed 9, 108–9
    embodied, 9, 105–6
    factors affecting, 105–6
    forms of, 9
    interoceptive sense and, 105
    reflecting on, 112
    situated, 9, 106–8
    types of, 104–9, 112, 113
cognitive flexibility
    described, 110
    nervous system flexibility
        underpinning, 98–113, 119
    reflecting on, 112
    in resilience, 110
cognitive load theory, 103–4
    reflecting on, 112
cognitive story
    ANS state impact on, 52
Cognitive Story Loop
    ANS state and, 28, 28f
    experiencing, 44
collective relationships
    described, 43

conflict(s)
    resolving, 72–73
connection(s)
    activities related to, 44–45
    in classroom, 65
    engagement from, 34–45, 118
    face-heart, 38
    learning foundation of, 27–45
    mind–body vs. mind–body–world, 98
    motivation from, 34–45, 118
    open-hearted, 38
    reflecting on, 44
    safety related to, 34–35, 41
    in ventral vagal state, 38
context
    defined, 40
    examples of providing, 40–41
    safety related to, 34–35, 40–41
co-regulated learning
    described, 55f, 56
co-regulating experiences
    in self-regulation management, 52
co-regulation, 8
    need for, 51
    safe, 51
    self-regulation following, 50–60, 118
Core SEL Competencies, 116
corpus callosum, 124
cultivate
    defined, 72
cultivation
    described, 73, 73f
curiosity
    dwell in, 118–24

Dana, D., xxiii–xxiv, 6–8, 13, 18, 79, 98,
    106
danger
    signals of, 35–36, 36f, 45
danger map(s), 64, 121
    drawing, 75
default mode, 79–80
    as freeze response, 87
    reflecting on, 93
default state, 8–9
Denworth, L., 13
disconnection
    situations creating, 64–65

disillusioned
  burned out vs., 12
distributed cognition, 108–9
  defined, 9
dorsal vagal state, 102–3, 102*f*
  Autonomic Ladder view from, 22–23
  described, 18, 18*f,* 20, 22–23
dorsal vagus pathway, 15*f,* 16–18, 18*f*
Dweck, C., 98–99, 101
dysregulation, 119–20
  co-, 51

education
  hemispheres of, 122–24
embodied cognition, 105–6
  defined, 9
emotion(s)
  academic. *see* academic emotion(s)
  during academic emotional learning
    phases, 60
emotional learning
  academic, 57–58, 57*f,* 58*f,* 60
emotional state(s)
  of learners, 58
energy
  ventral, 21
engagement
  safety and connection leading to,
    34–45, 118
everyday resilience, 62
evolving mindset
  described, 99, 102*f*
evolving mindset cycle, 98–103, 100*f,* 102*f*
"Expecting," 127
experience(s)
  co-regulating, 52
external protective factors
  examples of, 70

face-heart connection, 38
failing
  quietly, 87–88
failure acceptance
  to success, 92–93
failure avoidance
  to success, 92–93
failure–success gap
  bridging of, 88–91, 89*f*

fight-or-flight response, 16
fixed mindset
  described, 98–103, 100*f,* 102*f*
flexibility
  cognitive. *see* cognitive flexibility
  nervous system, 98–113, 119
  of staff, 113
freeze, 86–87
  reflecting on, 94
freeze response, 86–87
  default mode as, 87
  reflecting on, 94
Friendship, 13
friendship(s)
  importance of, 13–14
  through play and laughter, 84

gesturing
  movement and, 106
  prosody of speech assisted by, 105–6
glimmer(s), 68–69
  creating, 75
Gold, C. M., 61–62, 72
go-to place within, 79–80. *see also* default
    mode
  discovering, 95
  students', 95
Green Acres
  described, 47–50, 53–54, 61
growth mindset, 98–103, 100*f,* 102*f*
  ANS pathways and, 99
  in regulated ventral vagal state, 101,
    102*f*

Hamlet, 50
hand gesturing
  prosody of speech assisted by,
    105–6
Hansen, U. J., 122–23
Harvard Medical School, 85–86
Heart of Trauma, 52–53
hemisphere(s)
  of education, 122–24
hierarchy
  Autonomic Ladder in depicting, 17–23,
    18*f*
  defined, 8
  described, 17

high-risk situations
  examples of, 69
"home away from home," 79
human relationships
  messiness of, 72

immobilization
  through rest and digest, 16
inclination
  affective, 57
Indiana University
  Traumatic Stress Research Consortium
    at, 4
interactive play
  as "neural exercise," 82
interactive regulation, 8, 52–53, 59–60
internal protective factors
  examples of, 69–70
interoception
  described, 105–6
interoceptive sense
  as embodied cognitive resource,
    105
intimate relationships
  described, 43

Jennings, P., 12
joy
  through play, 82–84
joyful learning
  ventral path to, 97–113

Kain, K. L., 64
Keller, G., 4
kindness
  self-. see self-kindness
Kutlu, Ö., 110

laughter
  friendships through, 84
  play and, 84
learner(s)
  adaptable, 77–95. see also adaptable
    learners
  anchored, 77–95. see also anchor(s)
  emotional states of, 58
  regulated, 54–58, 55f, 57f, 58f. see also
    regulated learner(s)

learning
  academic emotional, 57–58, 57f, 58f, 60
  ANS impact on, 5–6
  blended states and, 81–88, 81f
  co-regulated, 55f, 56
  joyful, 97–113
  Polyvagal Theory as no-stress approach
    to, 7–9
  safe school environment in, 39
  socially shared regulation of, 55f, 56–57
  stages of, 55–56
  in state of play, 84
  stepping onto joyful path to, 43
learning foundation
  of safety and connection, 27–45. see
    also connection; safety
left hemisphere, 122–24
loneliness
  academic achievement impact of, 41–43
  creating project to remedy, 45
  described, 42
  solitude vs., 42
long-term memory
  working memory vs., 103–4

Mackesy, C., 24
map(s)
  danger, 64, 75, 121
map statement(s)
  Autonomic Ladder–related, 25
Martin, A. J., 89, 89f, 94
McGilchrist, I., 121–23
Mega, C., 57
memory(ies)
  long-term vs. working, 103–4
mending
  of misses, 62–63, 62f
metaphor(s)
  CLA-related, 33
mind–body connection
  mind–body–world connection vs., 98
mind–body–world connection
  mind–body connection vs., 98
mindfulness
  defined, 85
mindset(s). see also specific types, e.g.,
    growth mindset
  activities related to, 112–13

mindset(s) (*continued*)
    Autonomic Ladder and, 101–3, 102*f*
    as contextual, 99
    evolving, 99, 102*f*
    evolving cycle, 98–103, 100*f*, 102*f*
    fixed, 98–103, 100*f*, 102*f*
    growth, 98–103, 100*f*, 102*f*. *see also*
        growth mindset
    polyvagal-guided approach to, 98–103,
        100*f*, 102*f*
    Polyvagal Theory and, 98–113, 100*f*, 102*f*
    reflecting on, 111–12
    types of, 98–103, 100*f*, 102*f*. *see also*
        specific types, e.g., growth mindset
Mindset: The New Psychology of Success, 98
mismatch(es), 61–65, 62*f*
    breach and build, 62*f*, 63–65
    miss and mend, 62–63, 62*f*
    rupture and repair of, 62*f*, 63
    types of, 61–65
miss(es)
    impact of, 63
    mending of, 62*f*, 63
    on reparative continuum, 62–63, 62*f*
Mother Teresa, 23
motivation
    safety and connection leading to,
        34–45, 118
Motivation and Engagement Wheel, 88–
    91, 89*f*, 94, 101
movement
    gesturing and, 106
Murthy, V. H., 42
myths, metaphors, themes, stories layer
    in CLA, 30, 30*f*, 32–33

narrative(s)
    CLA and, 28–32, 28*f*, 30*f*
nervous system, 14–16, 15*f*
    activities related to, 25–26
    befriend your, 13–26. *see also* "befriend
        your nervous system"
    components of, 14–16, 15*f*. *see also*
        specific parts, e.g., autonomic
        nervous system (ANS)
    in determining how you feel about your
        work/personal life, 12

glimmers in monitoring, 68–69
overview of, 14–16, 15*f*
peripheral, 14–16, 15*f*
reactions of, 49–50
resilience through retuning, 66–75,
    118–19
role of, 98
somatic, 14–16, 15*f*
triggers in monitoring, 68–69
nervous system flexibility
    cognitive flexibility underpinned by,
        98–113, 119
nervous system state(s), 8–9. *see also*
    autonomic nervous system (ANS)
    state(s)
    during academic activities, 99–103, 102*f*
    awareness to, 105
    naming/addressing, 105
"neural exercise"
    interactive play as, 82
neuroception
    defined, 8, 35
neurodevelopmental interventions
    classroom use of, xxii–xxviii
New York Times, 24
"not enough time," 108
Nurturing Resilience, 64

observable behavior (litany) layer
    in CLA, 29–31, 30*f*
open-hearted connection, 38
Oxford English Dictionary
    on context, 40
    on cultivate, 72

parasympathetic nervous system, 15–17,
    15*f*
Paul, A. M., 97, 103
peripheral nervous system (PNS)
    described, 14–16, 15*f*
    motor division of, 14–16, 15*f*
    sensory division of, 14–16, 15*f*
play
    blended state of, 82
    described, 82
    evolution of, 84
    friendships through, 84

interactive, 82
joy through, 82–84
laughter from, 84
learning in, 84
reflecting on, 93–94
PNS. *see* peripheral nervous system (PNS)
polyvagal
defined, xxv
Polyvagal Learning Hub, 91–94, 91*f*, 101–3,
102*f*, 116
polyvagal lens
observing students through, 26
regulation through, 47–60. *see also* co-
regulation; regulated learner(s);
self-regulation
polyvagal principles for classroom, 115–24
Polyvagal Theory
academic resilience and, 69–71
ANS functions and, 4–6
becoming fluent in, 120–21
in "befriend your nervous system,"
13–26, 116. *see also* "befriend your
nervous system"
described, xxiii–xxiv, 4–7, 116–17
as evidence based, 6–7
mindsets and, 98–113, 100*f*, 102*f*. *see
also specific types and* mindset(s)
as no-stress approach to learning, 7–9
overarching concepts of, 17
promise of, 11–14
on resilience, 67
skills related to application in
classrooms, 73–74, 73*f*
viewing self-regulation through lens of
safety in, 51
Porges, S. W., xxiii, xxv, 4, 6, 35, 44, 51, 82
Polyvagal Theory of. *see* Polyvagal
Theory
possibility
dwell in, 118–24
productive learning
safe school environment in, 39
prosody of speech
hand gesturing role in, 105–6
protective factors
academic resilience supported by,
69–71

external, 70
internal, 69–70

quietly failing
described, 87–88
quietly failing response, 87–88
quietly still
blended state of, 85–86
reflecting on, 93–94
quotidian resilience, 62

Rae, L., xxiii
reality
resilience and, 61–75. *see also*
resilience
regulated learner(s)
co-regulated learning, 55*f*, 56
described, 54–58, 55*f*, 57*f*, 58*f*. *see also*
co-regulation; regulation; self-
regulation
self-regulated learning, 55–56, 55*f*
socially shared regulation of learning,
55*f*, 56–57
regulation
academic emotional learning, 57–58,
57*f*, 58*f*
activities related to, 59–60
co-. *see* co-regulation
interactive, 6, 52–53, 59–60
regulated learner(s), 54–58, 55*f*, 57*f*, 58*f*.
see also co-regulation; regulated
learner(s); self-regulation
self-. *see* self-regulation
through polyvagal lens, 47–60. *see also*
co-regulation; regulated learner(s);
self-regulation
relational relationships
described, 43
relationship(s)
collective, 43
dimensions of, 43
intimate, 43
messiness of, 72
reflecting on, 44
relational, 43
resilience and, 61–75. *see also* resilience
ruptures/mismatches in, 61

repair
  of ruptures, 62*f*, 63
reparative continuum, 61–65, 62*f*, 121
  activities related to, 75
  breaches on, 62*f*, 63–65. *see also*
    breach(es)
  mismatches on, 61–65, 62*f*. *see also*
    specific types and mismatch(es)
  misses on, 62–63, 62*f*
resilience, 61–75
  academic. *see* academic resilience
  activities related to, 75
  adaptability and, 78
  among students, 69
  cognitive flexibility in, 110
  development of, 62, 66–75
  everyday, 62
  Polyvagal Theory on, 67
  quotidian, 62
  reality and, 61–75
  reflecting on, 74
  relationships and, 61–75
  reparative continuum in, 61–65, 62*f*
  retuning nervous system in, 66–75,
    118–19
  safety rest stops in, 65–66
  shared, 66–67
resource(s)
  ventral, 78–95, 119. *see also* ventral
    resources
rest and digest
  immobilization through, 16
right hemisphere, 122–24
rudeness
  biological, 36–37
rupture(s), 61
  on reparative continuum, 62*f*, 63

safe school environment
  in productive learning, 39
safety
  academics and, 38–43. *see also* safety–
    academic link
  activities related to, 44–45
  engagement from, 34–45, 118
  learning foundation of, 27–45
  motivation from, 34–45, 118

observing signals of, 45
  reflecting on, 44
  in school environment, 39
  self-regulation through lens of, 51
  signals of, 35–38, 36*f*. *see also* safety
    signals
  three Cs of. *see* Three Cs of Safety
  through choices, 34–35, 39–40
  through connection, 34–35, 41
  through context, 34–35, 40–41
safety–academic link, 38–43
  loneliness impact on, 41–43
  safety through choices, 39–40
  safety through connection, 41
  safety through context, 40–41
safety rest stops
  drawing, 75
  in resilience, 65–66
safety scale, 35–36, 36*f*
safety signals
  from inside, 36–37
  between ourselves and others, 38
  from outside, 37
school environment
  safe, 39
S'cool Moves, xxii–xxiii
self-care
  in classroom, 23–24
self-kindness
  in classroom, 23–24
self-regulated learning
  described, 55–56, 55*f*
self-regulation
  co-regulating experiences in managing,
    52
  co-regulation and, 50–60, 118
  defined, 51, 60
  as learned skill, 51
  through lens of safety, 51
SEL perspective. *see* social-emotional
    learning (SEL) perspective
sense
  interoceptive, 105
sensory division
  of PNS, 14–16, 15*f*
Shakespeare, W., 50
shared resilience, 66–67

situated cognition, 106–8
  defined, 9
social bonding
  importance of, 13–14
social-emotional learning (SEL)
  perspective, 116
Social Engagement System(s), 67, 82, 106
  activation of, 50, 51
  described, 38
  miss impact on, 63
  pay attention to, 64
socially shared regulation of learning
  described, 55f, 56–57
Society for Psychophysiological Research,
  4
solitude
  described, 42
  loneliness vs., 42
somatic nervous system, 14–16, 15f
speech
  prosody of, 105–6
staff
  adaptability/flexibility of, 113
Stanford University, 99
state(s). *see also specific states and*
    autonomic nervous system (ANS)
    state(s)
  ANS responses as, 18–23, 18f
  blended. *see* blended state(s)
  default, 8–9
  emotional, 58
state of play
  learning in, 84
Stephens, R., xx–xxi
still
  quietly, 85–86, 93–94
student(s)
  go-to place within of, 95
  resilient vs. less resilient, 69
success
  from failure avoidance and acceptance
    to, 92–93
suck-swallow-breathe-vocalize synchrony,
  38
sympathetic nervous system, 15–17, 15f
sympathetic pathway, 17–18, 18f
sympathetic state, 101–2, 102f

Autonomic Ladder view from, 21–22
  described, 18–19, 18f, 21–22
systems layer
  in CLA, 30–31, 30f

Taylor, S., 13
"tend and befriend," 13
Terrell, S. J., 64
The Boy, the Mole, the Fox, and the Horse,
  24
*The Extended Mind: The Power of Thinking
  Outside the Brain,* 97
The Future of Smart, 122–23
*The Left Brain Speaks, the Right Brain
  Laughs,* xx–xxi
*The Master and His Emissary: The Divided
  Brain and the Making of the Western
  World,* 121
The One Thing, 4
theory
  defined, 6
The Pocket Guide to the Polyvagal Theory, 7
*The Polyvagal Theory in Therapy: Engaging
  the Rhythm of Regulation,* xxiv
The Power of Discord, 61–62
Three Cs of Safety, 6, 39–41, 106
  described, 34–35
  in emotional states of learners, 58
  reflecting on, 44
Together, 42
transformation
  CLA-related, 32–34
Traumatic Stress Research Consortium
  at Indiana University, 4
trigger(s), 68–69
  creating, 75
Tronick, E., 61–62, 72

University of New South Wales, Australia,
  89

vagal brake
  in action, 81
  adaptability and, 80
  described, 80
vagus
  defined, 16

vagus nerve
    described, 15–16, 15*f*
vagus nerve fibers
    described, 16
ventral anchor(s)
    examples of, 77–78
    reflecting on, 93
    ventral resources as, 78–79
ventral energy, 21
ventral path
    to joyful learning, 97–113
ventral replay
    activity related to, 59–60
ventral resources
    in adaptability, 78–95, 119. *see also*
        ventral anchor(s)
    discovering, 78–79
ventral vagal anchor chart

creating, 94
ventral vagal state
    Autonomic Ladder view from, 21
    connection in, 38
    described, 18–19, 18*f,* 21, 101
    growth mindset in, 101, 102*f*
ventral vagus pathway, 15*f,* 16–18, 18*f*

Wall Street Journal, 2
What to Expect the First Year, 127
Wheel of Awareness, 116
Willard, C., 85–86
Wilson, Shalea, xix–xxi, 42–43, 66, 82, 87,
    125–127
working memory
    long-term memory vs., 103–4

Yavuz, H. Ç., 110

About the Author

Dr. Debra Em Wilson is a reading specialist, educational consultant, and founder of S'cool Moves, Inc. She earned her doctorate from the University of Southern Queensland Professional Studies Program. Her teaching experience includes high school biology, literacy coaching K–12, and college health courses. Dr. Wilson's consulting practice focuses on enhancing collaboration between general and special education. She's a mother of two, including a daughter with special needs. Dr. Wilson enjoys honing her skills as a certified color and design consultant, swimming in her saltwater pool, and biking through the beautiful Sonoran Desert in Tucson, Arizona.